DATE DUE

SINCLAIR LEWIS

A BIOGRAPHICAL SKETCH BY
CARL VAN DOREN

SINCLAIR LEWIS

SINCLAIR LEWIS

A Biographical Sketch

By
CARL VAN DOREN

With a Bibliography by
HARVEY TAYLOR

KENNIKAT PRESS
Port Washington, N. Y./London

CONTENTS

	PAGE
PRELIMINARY	1
I. CRAFT	7
II. MAN	29
III. CRAFTSMAN	50
CHRONOLOGY	71
BIBLIOGRAPHY, by Harvey Taylor	79

SINCLAIR LEWIS

PRELIMINARY

IN THE four years since *Dodsworth* Sinclair Lewis
has not published a new novel. Prophets have
croaked and cawed that he would never write
another. His decade, they have pointed out, is
dead. The ten years which began with *Main Street*
in 1920 ended in 1930 with the award of the Nobel
Prize. Historians have filed him away with the
classics, arguing about the shelf on which he belonged. The communists among his critics have
discovered that he was middle class. The run of
Americans who felt the pickle of his satire have
come to wonder if their lash was after all so stinging
as they first thought. Even those who laughed with
him have some of them learned the lesson too well
and have got to taking him more or less for granted.
He has become a contemporary phenomenon about
which too many minds have decided that they were
made up.

It was, consequently, time for Mr. Lewis to
disturb such smug conclusions. *Ann Vickers* will

disturb them. Here again is the green, springing energy which has marked all his work. Once more he has chosen a large theme and has done large justice to it. Apparently as erudite a specialist as in *Arrowsmith* or *Elmer Gantry*, he has made himself at home, and takes his readers home with him, in the gray world of charity, the black world of prisons. While adding dozens of minor persons, all individualized and recognizable, to the long list of his characters, he has told another full life story which puts Ann Vickers in her due place beside Carol Kennicott and George F. Babbitt and Martin Arrowsmith and Elmer Gantry and Samuel Dodsworth. Where before he had five major novels he now has six.

If comparisons are to be made, *Ann Vickers* is perhaps nearer to *Arrowsmith* than to any of the others. Ann is one of Mr. Lewis's heroes. Carol Kennicott is occasionally foolish, Babbitt frequently absurd, Elmer Gantry egregious and outrageous; Samuel Dodsworth is a man watched through a crisis, not followed through a long evolving period. But Ann is the female counterpart of Arrowsmith. She has knowledge, will, force. She aspires, she persists, she succeeds. At every point she has Mr. Lewis's evident approval, based upon an insight which he has not hitherto revealed where women were concerned. Even Leora Arrowsmith and Fran Dodsworth are hardly more than triumphant sketches of women, one very simple and faithful, the other very complex and false. Ann Vickers is a scrupulous portrait and a thorough history of a woman. Her story has the body and substance, the diversity and range, which fiction has commonly exhibited only in its men. No doubt most readers of her story will see that Ann has been studied through very masculine eyes. That was to be expected from Sinclair Lewis. It is likely that the book will reawaken the fervor of controversy which has attended Mr. Lewis's whole career. That too was to be expected.

There will be, almost certainly, two principal grounds of controversy. The first will have to do with the social documents in the case. Are American prisons as bad as Mr. Lewis represents them? Ought they or ought they not to be like this? The second will have to do with the personal fortunes of the heroine. Can a woman give herself to her profession as a man gives himself to his? Are her work and her love compatible? Do all her roads bend back, or do they not, to one overwhelming necessary end? Are feminists feminine? These are the issues of debate which can be readily foreseen, with their cross-fire and smoke and echoes. But there may be others. It is never possible to know in advance all the discussion that a new novel by Sinclair Lewis will provoke. He has felt ground tremors of opinion and sentiment before even he could think them out and analyze them.

For this reason it is impossible to measure and weigh one of his novels before it has been published. The receptions which his various books have had are a part of his biography. His biography is a part of recent history. No man can yet say more of *Ann Vickers* than that it is in the main line of Mr. Lewis's achievement. It has still to make its way, rouse its din, exert its influence, and settle into its eventual position as the life story of one of those men and women who have been created to outlast this age.

Meanwhile consider the previous adventures of Sinclair Lewis and his earlier books.

SINCLAIR LEWIS

I. CRAFT

SINCLAIR LEWIS stood up like a restless, determined, tall flame. He was at Stockholm in December, 1930, and, having just been given the Nobel Prize in Literature, he was the most conspicuous American man of letters living. For weeks his name had had its daily place in the headlines of two continents and more. His countrymen, pleased that the honor had at last fallen to the first American, were touchily uncertain that this American deserved it. A satirist, as they called him, he had killed sacred cows, washed native linen before the eyes of the world, fouled his own nest, discredited a fatherland. Provincials shivered. Patriots thought up loud irrelevances. Only in Stockholm, innocent center of the storm, was there enough quiet to let the winner of the prize be heard. Even in the grave presence of the Swedish Academy he had to raise his voice, he felt, above the mutterings beyond the Atlantic.

About himself he said little but that he was grateful and had always been fortunate. As if the prize had come to his "greatly beloved land," "the most contradictory, the most depressing, the most stirring" country in the world, rather than to any single writer, he spoke of a whole literature, with a "complete and unguarded frankness" which was his tribute to the audience and the occasion. Some other American, almost any other American, might have used the tongue of ambassadors. Mr. Lewis with a blunt integrity told his hearers, and the waiting newspapers, that the literature of the United States still lagged behind the hopes of its friends and prophets.

"In America," he said, "most of us—not readers alone but even writers—are still afraid of any literature which is not a glorification . . . of our faults as well as our virtues. . . . We still most revere the writers for the popular magazines who in a hearty and edifying chorus chant that the America of a hundred and twenty million population is still as simple, as pastoral, as it was when it had but forty million; . . . that . . . America has gone through the revolutionary change from rustic colony to world-empire without having in the least altered the bucolic and Puritanic simplicity of Uncle Sam."

Mr. Lewis called names. Suppose, he said, the Swedish Academy had given the prize to Theodore Dreiser, "who has cleared the trail from . . .

timidity and gentility in American fiction to honesty and boldness and passion of life," seeming when he first came to "housebound and airless America like a great free Western wind"; or had given the prize to Eugene O'Neill, "who has done nothing much in American drama save to transform it utterly, in ten or twelve years, from a false world of neat and competent trickery to a world of splendor and fear and greatness"; or had given the prize to James Branch Cabell, Willa Cather, H. L. Mencken, Sherwood Anderson, Upton Sinclair, Joseph Hergesheimer, or Ernest Hemingway. If the Swedish Academy had made any of these choices, there would have been uproar in America. Numerous Americans, not recognizing their face in such mirrors, would have seen in the award an insult to their nation.

"The American novelist or poet or dramatist or sculptor or painter must work alone, in confusion, unassisted save by his integrity. . . . He is oppressed ever . . . by the feeling that what he creates does not matter, that he is expected by his readers to be only a decorator or a clown, or that he is good-naturedly accepted as a scoffer whose bark probably is worse than his bite and who probably is a good fellow at heart, who in any case certainly does not count in a land that produces eighty-story buildings, motors by the million, and wheat by the billions of bushels. And he has no institution, no group, to which he can turn for inspiration, whose criticism he can accept and whose praise will be precious to him."

Mr. Lewis went on calling names. The American Academy, he told the Swedish Academy, did have among its members Nicholas Murray Butler, Wilbur Cross, Edwin Arlington Robinson, Robert Frost, James Truslow Adams, Edith Wharton, Hamlin Garland, Owen Wister, Brand Whitlock, Booth Tarkington. But it did not have Theodore Dreiser, H. L. Mencken, George Jean Nathan, Eugene O'Neill, Edna St. Vincent Millay, Carl Sandburg, Robinson Jeffers, Vachel Lindsay, Edgar Lee Masters, Willa Cather, Joseph Hergesheimer, Sherwood Anderson, Ring Lardner, Ernest Hemingway, Louis Bromfield, Wilbur Daniel Steele, Fannie Hurst, Mary Austin, James Branch Cabell, Edna Ferber, Upton Sinclair. Some of the Academy's exclusions might be accidents and some might mean that eligible writers had refused or would refuse election. "I should not expect any Academy to be so fortunate as to contain all these writers, but one which fails to contain any of them, which thus cuts itself off from so much of what is living and vigorous and original in American letters, can have no relationship whatever to our life and aspirations. It does not represent literary America of today—it represents only Henry Wadsworth Longfellow."

The American Academy, Mr. Lewis told the eager newspapers, was a perfect example "of the divorce in America of intellectual life from all authentic standards of importance and reality." The American universities, rich in social prestige, throbbing with athletics, and hospitable to science, were in the arts "far from reality and living creation." "To a true-blue professor of literature in an American university, literature is not something that a plain human being, living today, painfully sits down to produce. . . . Our American professors like their literature clear and cold and pure and very dead." No doubt a similar necrolatry might be found in European universities. "But in the new and vital and experimental land of America, one would expect the teachers of literature to be less monastic, more human, than in the traditional shadows of old Europe. They are not." Nothing warmer had recently come from the American universities than the "chilly enthusiasms of the New Humanists," into "a world so exciting and promising as this today, a life brilliant with Zeppelins and Chinese revolutions and the Bolshevik industrialization of farming and ships and the Grand Canyon and young children and terrifying hunger and the lonely quest of scientists after God."

Nor was there in America, the relentless chauvinist declared, any great critic or school of criticism helpful to creative writers. "America has never had a Brandes, a Taine, a Goethe, a Croce. . . . Our Erasmuses have been village schoolmistresses." The American standard of literary excellence had been set by William Dean Howells, who was "one of the gentlest, sweetest, and most honest of men," but "who had the code of a pious old maid whose greatest delight was to have tea at the vicarage." With his soft strength he had tamed Mark Twain, "perhaps the greatest of our writers," and had "put that fiery old savage into an intellectual frock coat and top hat." He had subdued Hamlin Garland, "who should in every way have been greater than Howells but who under Howells' influence was changed from a harsh and magnificent realist into a genial and insignificant lecturer."

"And so, without standards, we have survived." Mr. Lewis would not follow his logic to despair. "And for the strong young men, it has perhaps been well that we should have no standards. For, after seeming to be pessimistic about my own and much beloved land, I want to close this dirge with a very lively sound of optimism. I have, for the future of American literature, every hope and every eager belief. . . . There are young Americans today who are doing such passionate and authentic work that it makes me sick to see that I am a little too old to be one of them." He ended with a last calling of names: Ernest Hemingway, Thomas Wolfe,

Thornton Wilder, John Dos Passos, Stephen Benét, Michael Gold, William Faulkner. "I salute them, with a joy in being not yet too far removed from their determination to give to the America that has mountains and endless prairies, enormous cities and lost far cabins, billions of money and tons of faith, to an America that is as strange as Russia and as complex as China, a literature worthy of her vastness."

Cables whispered under the Atlantic, and America bristled. Sinclair Lewis had turned his hornets loose again. He had mocked the Academy, the universities, the New Humanists. He had cast down venerable names and had called young names into prominence. With his drastic idiom he had disturbed a stately ceremony. On a day when he should have been suave with general praise and compliment, he had, the charges ran, paid off old scores, amused himself with paradox, cantankerously missed all his marks, stirred up wrath for fun, or—of course—hunted and caught publicity. The winner of the Nobel prize was still Sinclair Lewis.

He was still Sinclair Lewis. No stranger mystery lay back of his behavior. He had, by nature and by instinct, always burningly demanded that human life be beautiful and splendid; always been disappointed that he could not everywhere find what his passion looked for; always offset his anger at stupidity by his delight in comedy; always spoken without muffling his words. His address before the Swedish Academy was as characteristic as any of his novels. The man who had, somehow, expected that the American Academy and the universities and the New Humanists could be sensitive, powerful friends to creative literature, and had felt compelled to own that they were not, was the man who had expected that prairie villages could be aspiring, minor business men profound, bull-necked evangelists just and lowly, and had been driven to the truth about them. His speech had been, no matter what anybody said, almost amusingly American. Though he had condemned many of the low houses which his country's literature had built, he had done it in the interest of sky-scrapers now building, and in the face of all his arguments he had predicted other skyscrapers which would some day cast their shadows to both oceans. The satirist had actually been patriotic and grandiose.

The angry critics of his speech lost themselves in its details. They sided with or against the whipped Academicians, professors of literature, New Humanists. They weighed this or that name which had received his praise. Without holding back their judgments till they could know just what he had said, and all of it, they read the first summarized reports and made up hasty minds

about him. On most sides it was agreed that he had
spoken with inadequate decorum, and that he had,
by craftily bringing on the thunders of the press,
once more attracted to himself the congenial spotlight.

Decorums differ. If Mr. Lewis had been a member of the American Academy or a professor of
literature, he might becomingly have saluted the
academies and universities of Europe in the name
of literate America and might have expressed his
gratitude in congratulations. If he had gone to
Sweden in a uniform of diplomacy he might have
thought it his duty to point out how greatly his
country deserved the recognition which it so greatly
valued. Mr. Lewis was only an American man of
letters who had won an international prize. On this
day his critical opinions would carry farther than
they ever had before or ever would again. He knew
he must not, like an official, stiffen his speech with
platitudes. He took America, literature, and himself too seriously to be willing to misrepresent any
of them. The occasion would lose all its strategic
value if he smothered it with commonplaces. His
highest tact would be to tell the truth.

He told all he knew and had time for in his brief
address. Not too much of what he said was novel.
Observant critics had made most of his points
before him. Some of his strictures were not above
debate, and some of his generosities were hardly

warranted. But, thanks to his position as well as to his genius, he was writing on the sky what other critics had merely uttered in shop-talk or buried in literary journals. The wonder was, not that he should say such things, but that he should say them on so reverberating a rostrum, without the careful silences or evasions which might have been excused as nothing worse than courtesy. And so the wonder was only that he was Sinclair Lewis, whose craft has always consisted in speaking out what others grumbled.

There was, inevitably, the charge that he had chosen these words for this occasion to draw still more of the world's eyes upon himself. That vulgarest of indictments, seldom brought by any but the mean and envious, was not new to Mr. Lewis. For ten years he had lived under it. Because his sayings and doings got into the newspapers, it was perversely argued that he said and did things for the sake of getting there. The explanation that he was always interesting news had been too often overlooked, and the fact that there had been for him as much bitter as sweet in his celebrity. It would have been as accurate to say that he got into the newspapers because he had acted as if there were no newspapers to get into. He had neither courted them nor feared them. This seems to have been almost beyond the understanding of those who were, and are, themselves not indifferent to

newspapers. But it is not beyond human understanding.

Consider the three occasions which have marked
the name of Sinclair Lewis with the noisiest re-
nown. The first was when he declined the Pulitzer
prize awarded to *Arrowsmith*; the second, when he
dared God, as it is innocently remembered, to strike
him dead in a pulpit in Kansas City; the third,
when he won the Nobel prize and was a critic for
an hour.

The Pulitzer prize for "the American novel
published during the year which shall best present
the wholesome atmosphere of American life and
the highest standard of American manners and
manhood" was nine years old in 1926. Although the
terms of the award were fatuous, the awarding
committees had by their choices made it guessable
that they believed they were selecting the best
novel of each year, falling back upon the Pulitzer
description only when they needed a support in
their own prejudices. Their judgments had been
frequently if not systematically bad. Critical as
well as moral standards might have led them to
give the prize to *The Age of Innocence* over *Main
Street*, *Miss Lulu Bett*, *Moon-Calf*, *Figures of Earth*,
100%, and *This Side of Paradise*, or to *Alice Adams*
over *Three Soldiers*, or to *One of Ours* over *Babbitt*
and *Peter Whiffle* and *Cytherea*. But they had
preferred *His Family* (by Ernest Poole) to *The*

Three Black Pennys, and *The Magnificent Ambersons* to *My Antonia*, and *The Able McLaughlins* (by Margaret Wilson) to *A Lost Lady* and *Escapade* and *Jennifer Lorn* and *The High Place*. They had made no award for the famous year of *Jurgen*.

Here was proof that the Pulitzer committees had been taking something into account besides literary excellence. Wholesomeness, however, was not all that had deflected them. They had leaned also towards mediocrity, with the prudence of academic amateurs drawn into judicial huddles. Critics had annually remarked the tendency of the awards, but the public had been unable to hear in the din of reputation which the prizes brought. Nobody, it seemed, could do anything. Mr. Lewis could and did. When the Pulitzer prize was awarded to *Arrowsmith* he rejected both the honor and the money.

He gave serious reasons for his stand, declaring that he thought little of literary prizes in general and less than little of the Pulitzer prize in particular. Hardly any attention was paid to what he said. His true reasons were found for him by all the gossips. They supposed that he had been cross-grained in order to become conspicuous; that he had denied himself the prize for the sake of many times its value in notoriety; that he had economically got even with the Pulitzer committees for passing over *Main Street* and *Babbitt*; that he was, in short, a crafty politician. What the gossips overlooked was that Mr. Lewis had not merely argued, but had acted. No doubt he foresaw everything that might be said about his action and all the advantages which would come to him along with the misapprehensions and insults. He must even have expected that some of his friends, the timid ones, would wonder whether he was not taking a Pulitzer prize too solemnly by making a stir about it. But such foreknowledge could not deter him. He had an impulse to do a thing and the courage to do it though it was simple and original.

Another novelist, who had formerly won and accepted the Pulitzer prize, is said to have envied Mr. Lewis his master stratagem. Some later prizewinners must have wished, helplessly, that they could do more than envy. But beforehand was too early, since the idea had not yet been born, and afterwards was too late, since the credit now would all go back to him. Simplicity and originality are more than strategy. They are unpredictable, inimitable essentials. No matter what may happen, Adam must remain the first man. And Mr. Lewis must remain the first man who ever made a literary prize a nine-days' tempest in the American press. His craft was pure nature. He was simply and originally himself, and the endless argument flowed from that mysterious fact.

So with his reputed challenge to Jehovah. It is

ordinarily imagined that he thrust himself into a pulpit, defied God, and held up long hands in a blasphemous invitation to the lightning—his eyes meanwhile studying the reporters. Nothing is less like the occasion or the man. He was at the time in Kansas City at work on a novel which was to be the life story of a clergyman. Asked to speak at a gathering in a church, he touched upon a silly legend which at the moment had some currency among the superstitious. Luther Burbank, the legend said, had doubted the existence of God and had soon after died of God's wrath. Mr. Lewis sensibly pointed out that as Burbank had been an old man, with hardened arteries, he might have died as soon in any case, and that there was no scientific proof that his skepticism had caused his end. To make a surer test of the penalties of doubt, Mr. Lewis offered himself. Here before witnesses, in a church, he would say that he disbelieved, and would give God ten minutes in which to show His anger. God did not take the matter up. It was the newspapers that replied.

Far from having planned the hurly-burly, Mr. Lewis was startled by it. He had been engaged in an experiment to disprove a superstition. In a reasonable world his act could have meant no more than that. In this world what he had done was taken to be outrageous or, at best, boisterous. He had committed blasphemy. He had disturbed the peace. He had been unkind to the devout. He had shown bad manners and bad taste. He had done it all for the publicity it would bring him. Nowhere does it seem to have been perceived that he had only carried out a realistic test in a natural way. Simplicity and originality look melodramatic because they look larger than life. But it is the smaller people who see the melodrama in them.

The Nobel prize address was in the same line of passionate, frank courage as the Pulitzer blasphemy and the Kansas City snub. So are the three novels, *Main Street*, *Babbitt*, and *Elmer Gantry*, which most among Mr. Lewis's books have beat up incidental game.

To read *Main Street* after a dozen years is to wonder what has become of the vitriol it was said to spray in 1920. The texts which were then torn from their pages and fought over now turn out to be infrequent and hardly controvertible. Of course small communities are set in their small habits. Of course a restive young woman finds it difficult to slow down to an unadventurous gait and to accept the wisdom of her village elders. Emma Bovary had illustrated that more than a half-century, and Emma Woodhouse more than a century, before Carol Kennicott. *Main Street* was an American variation on a classic theme. It was, from the first, no less classic because Mr. Lewis had, when he was twenty and restive, already observed in himself and in his village the possibilities of antagonism, and had planned a novel on the Village Virus which was to take the lawyer Guy Pollock for the hero and to trace his infection and undoing. The autobiography behind that unwritten novel gave some of the passionate authenticity to the rebellion of Carol Kennicott, when she had ousted Pollock from the first place in the narrative. To be authentic is a way to become classic. *Main Street* even in 1920 was only an honest story told without regard to consequences.

There were, however, sudden consequences. A pattern of thought had been violated. The American village had been, in American fiction, seldom touched by the vigorous hands of realism. It seemed, says an earlier observer, "too cosy a microcosm to be disturbed. There it lay in the mind's eye, neat, compact, organized, traditional: the white church with tapering spire, the sober schoolhouse, the smithy of the ringing anvil, the corner grocery, the cluster of friendly houses; the venerable parson, the wise physician, the canny squire, the grasping landlord softened or outwitted in the end; the village belle, gossip, atheist, idiot; jovial fathers, gentle mothers, merry children; cool parlors, shining kitchens, spacious barns, lavish gardens, fragrant summer dawns, and comfortable winter evenings." No matter what a reader's own experience might have been with the villages he knew, he had learned to look in novels for this beguiling pattern, and to withhold his sympathies from the characters who did not fit it. They were rogues or fools, or else misguided youngsters who would come to their senses when they had tried their silly wings and found them useless.

Across this familiar pattern Mr. Lewis rode on a high horse. His Gopher Prairie was dusty, frowsy, smug, intolerant of changes because incapable of seeing that any change could brighten it. His Carol Kennicott was not, romantically, a genius. He knew that a girl of genius would, even from Gopher Prairie, have been drawn away to the footlights and fleshpots—the privacy and the kind anonymity—of a more shining neighborhood. Carol was barely superior to the village level in her gifts, except for her virtue of discontent. At the last she yielded like any classic heroine struggling against her environment. But she held, and Mr. Lewis agreed with her, that her discontent had been virtue, not crime or folly. The villain of the piece had been the dullness of Gopher Prairie.

This plain story and its plain application were too plain to be received for what they were. Thousands who had suffered from their villages rose to shouts of triumphant recognition and turned missionary. Tens of thousands who had not felt dull in their villages defended them and any like them. Rival prejudices, having found in the book

a cause for war, read it chiefly to pick up ammu-
nition. *Main Street*, made a flag and target, became
a symbol, and was blamed for all the war's ex-
cesses. But they are actually not in the book itself.
Or if they are, they are largely implicit there, like
all the controversial ideas which are set loose when
a story runs a straight course without regard to
customary deviations, or when a human being
persists in living his life in the straight line of a
powerful individuality.

When *Babbitt* followed *Main Street* the contro-
versialists were ready. Once more they weltered
in prejudices. There were accepted patterns for the
American business man in fiction, ranging from
those of Horatio Alger to those of Theodore Dreiser,
but generally displaying him as a type and almost
always moralizing him, whether with a naïve
hero-worship or with a kind of monastic censure
for his addiction to the world. The story of George
F. Babbitt neither marveled nor condemned.
Babbitt had not risen by following the maxims
of the copybooks. He had more or less blundered
into such success as he had had, in a profession
which had not been his first choice, with a wife
whom mere accident had selected for him. Having
no thoroughgoing character of his own, and never
having needed one to survive, he had become an
expert in protective coloration. In the clan of the
realtors he was as indistinguishable as any bee in

any hive. But in him, as in Carol Kennicott, there was a germ of distinction. The misfortunes of a friend, who had fallen out of step with the tribe, forced Babbitt to consider his own submergence. A disturbing love affair made him pay more attention to his emotional life than he had ever done before. Little as the leaven was, it stirred in him. For a time he struggled to be himself, vaguely aware what his separate self was. And though he soon turned back to the rhythm of his clan, he had been, in his small way, a hero.

The story Mr. Lewis told is all that persists in the book after a quarreling decade. But in 1922 it was too simple to be left to its original mystery. Innumerable critics of American life pounced upon the character of Babbitt as evidence that the typical American was something geometrical and automatic, good only for being squared and settled into the flat national design. The fact of his rebellion went unnoticed, or else was called a further evidence of his triviality. He had been an ineffectual malcontent, an unpersevering lover. And he could not be blamed, since American life in general was what it was. The patriots responded with points likewise distant from the issue. Whatever the arguments on either side, they were seldom about Babbitt. His name became as proverbial as Main Street, but his nature was misread or, more often, entirely overlooked. He was less a man than a label. He paid a singular price for going through a classic experience, that of the man of action and property who hesitates in his career and dubiously weighs his possessions. Yet this is not too singular a fortune for a classic theme. Mr. Lewis, telling the familiar story with such outward freshness that the fable itself seemed a new invention, had the advantage of a plot which, like every first-hand adventure of the intellect or the emotions, is as usual and yet as original as a child just born.

Elmer Gantry was a third challenge to a pattern. The United States, for all its unwillingness to let the churches meddle with the government, has been kind, if not soft, towards religions in general. They have had no anti-clerical party to contend with, and only a few outspoken enemies. Clergymen, and particularly clergymen in fiction, have been regarded as somehow beyond realism, benevolent lay-figures engaged in honorable though slightly mystifying rites. Most American novelists seem to have taken their clergymen on faith out of a tradition. Mr. Lewis, acutely up-to-date, knew that the twentieth century in America had developed, in the absence of criticism, clergymen who were brawling bellwethers of their flocks, wily, fleshly, unimaginative, arrogant. They might not be numerous, but they did exist. *Elmer Gantry* was the life story of one of them.

The outcry which greeted it might have been hysterical if the public had not been prepared for anything from Sinclair Lewis. For this, even he had not quite prepared them. The arguments which came to them while they read blinded them to the story which he had written. He must, they felt, be meaning to say that all clergymen are abominable. He must be attacking the very foundations of the churches. In such a cause no novelist could be disinterested. This was not drama but debate. Debaters took up arms. At some points Mr. Lewis gave color to the charge that he had stepped outside his direct path of narrative. Certain of his phrases sounded too much like H. L. Mencken, and one of his episodes too much, or not enough, like James Branch Cabell. The story-teller could not hide his anger at a clergyman who was a bully, a sneak, a liar, a lecher, a drunkard, and an ignoramus. And yet this was essentially a story, and a classic story, of a false priest who himself committed the sins he scourged in others. Mr. Lewis had once more chosen a large theme, given it substance out of sharp-eyed experience and observation, and then handled it in his own imperious, regardless way.

With three stormy actions and three peculiarly controverted novels in a dozen years Mr. Lewis has been, in effect, a biennial irritant to the United States. It is time, however, to perceive that though resulting scandals buzz around his name, his character begins to emerge from them in its right proportions. Those snarling questions whether he was good or bad, right or wrong, wise or foolish, considerate or rude, yield to the important questions, which in the long run are all that last, whether he was strong or weak, interesting or tedious, something or nothing. He has been strong, interesting, something. These, far more than the cunning with which he has been credited, and far more than his apparent luck, are his secrets. His craft has been, and is, only to be simply, originally himself, and to tell the life stories of the men and women who have from time to time laid hold on his driving, driven imagination.

II. MAN

SINCLAIR LEWIS is the quintessence of the United States, set off by a special genius but not transmuted from the general type. Those inquiring foreigners who in the eighteenth century would have sought out Benjamin Franklin as the essential American, or in the nineteenth, Mark Twain, would in the twentieth find what they were looking for in Sinclair Lewis. If the United States were rich enough, it might well endow him as a permanent exhibit in whom philosophical visitors could study the national epitome.

As to flesh and blood, Mr. Lewis has the long, heroic angularity of Uncle Sam, the color of a torch, the mobile impatience which comes from quick and restless nerves. In any imaginable society he would be as noticeable as a bashful cyclone. He enters a room with a diffident insolence, bracing himself against what lies in wait for him. After all his harsh campaigns, he has still an eager, shy desire to please. Even while, in the high voice of a tall man, he talks with this person or that small group, his darting eyes watch every other possible observer. Those who know him least imagine he is demanding admiration. Those who know him best understand he is only hoping for affection. Surrounded by bores, he soon withers, flinging out, over their earnest heads, wordless pleas for help. Escaped to friends, Mr. Lewis may be as robust as Babbitt in his greetings. He laughs freely, in a tone nearer a neigh than a roar, a bark, a mew, or a hiss. His talk is a torrent, almost never narrative. He does not tell anecdotes or offer reminiscences. He changes the subject so rapidly as sometimes to confuse slower speakers, who do not know that he has already found out all they have to say about it. He does not, however, interrupt others to spring his own epigrams. He is not epigrammatical. He talks personalities, but does not lose himself in long discussions of any single person. There are two things which, in conversation, he does best. One is to work out the full details of some ridiculous project, such as an Academy of Illiterates, naming the eligible members and assigning them to their ranks and titles. The other is to mimic some pretentious fool, preferably one showing off in public. Mr. Lewis's mimicry is amazing, largely vocal. He tries, not to look the rôle he is playing, but to sound it. Himself to the eye, to the ear he can be any human noise at will.

His talent for mimicry is perhaps a symptom. Experience has not insulated him with protective callus. His senses are eternally on guard. He cannot be inattentive without being unconscious. Conscious, he is a man without a skin. That is, he seems to wear a skin which is all eyes, all ears, all nerves of sense. Life beats on him like suns, drums, hammers; like searchlights, calliopes, stinging nettles. Small irritations make him fractious. Crowds wear him out. New York disintegrates him. At the end of even a brief season in Manhattan he is a lank, flushed Hercules in a poisoned shirt. But the trouble must lie hardly deeper than his skin, for a few days at his farm in Vermont will quiet him again.

Most men so sensitive turn hermit. Mr. Lewis has no longer—if he ever had—a gift for loneliness. Too little sensation is as bad for him as too much. In his earliest novels and in his latest, in his account of Samuel Dodsworth no less than of William Wrenn, loneliness is terror and torment. Whatever other states of mind and nerves Mr. Lewis may have studied in the lives of his characters, he has come back most often to loneliness and has revealed in his handling of it the most exact, the most diverse sympathy. It is a sympathy of knowledge, a knowledge of experience. Nature does not abhor a vacuum more than Mr. Lewis abhors a day empty of some kind of companionship. In the country, working, he is lost unless he has a friendly ear within call. He greets endurable visitors with a hospitality that is almost an appetite, and he makes them feel guilty as well as regretful when they must leave. No matter with what scratches or wounds he may withdraw from society, he is forced to it again by a compulsion as incurable as his sensitiveness.

The concurrence of touchy nerves and hungry energy is what produces the chief American characteristics. Few Americans are thick-skinned enough to cultivate eccentricity, welcome criticism, resign themselves to abstract, solitary contemplation, or fatalistically weigh gains and losses. Most Americans rush into action without thinking why, and prefer activity to peace because of habits, not of reasons. Mr. Lewis, essentially American, has not been spared the conflict in himself which comes from the national ambivalence. Genius has given him a voice, but it is his conflict which has kept him in the center of so many frays from which his thin skin has borne away so many wincing records.

Geographically Mr. Lewis more or less sums up America. His father's father left Connecticut for California in the gold rush and got back with nothing. His mother's father, born in Virginia, returned from Canada to be a surgeon in the Union army during the Civil War. His own father was a New Englander and a country doctor in the Middle West. Mr. Lewis himself was born in Minnesota in 1885, had his schooling there and in Ohio, and went to Yale. Not yet quite content at Yale, he not only made two orthodox summer voyages on cattle boats to England, but left the university altogether in what would have been his final year. He looked for an intenser, richer life at Helicon Hall, in New Jersey, as Hawthorne had looked for it in the earlier communistic experiment at Brook Farm, and found himself as dissatisfied as Hawthorne. He tried free-lancing in a New York slum. He traveled steerage to Panama to get a job, and failed. Back at Yale for an actual last year, he was tempted to weaken and become a doctor of philosophy. Instead, being strong and greedy for experience, he became an editor on a small newspaper in Iowa; then a charity worker in New York; then—having crossed the continent in a day coach —a part-time secretary in California, and later, in turn, reporter in San Francisco; then—back across the continent—an assistant editor in Washington of a magazine for teachers of the deaf; then, at twenty-five, once more in New York, to begin five years of hack work for publishers until he had married, published two novels, and been made independent by the favor of the *Saturday Evening Post*. During another five years he lived in Florida, Chicago, his native village of Sauk Centre, motored

from Minnesota to the Pacific Coast, came back by
the Grand Canyon and New Orleans to New York,
spent a summer in Cape Cod and a winter in
Minneapolis, threw off two popular novels and one
more serious, and, giving rein to an old impulse,
stayed long enough in Washington to write *Main
Street*, after which, at thirty-five, he discovered
that he had held up to America the mirror which
he did not know he was. Since then he has been, in
the United States, Canada, the Caribbean, Europe,
as nomadic as Mark Twain, has been divorced
and remarried, and has settled in Vermont on the
first land he ever owned. He thinks that he has
settled there, but he is still as restless as America,
and nobody can foresee on what expeditions he
may go, how long he may stay, or when or whether
he will return.

On none of these imperative adventures has Mr.
Lewis been a vague romantic, running after blue
birds or hunting for blue flowers. Such fantasies did
not outlast his boyhood, when first they took a
familiar form of resentment because Minnesota
had no Robin Hoods, no Ivanhoes, no clanging
tournaments and solemn castles. This first resentment having passed, he formed another because
Yale was not the suave, mellow, glowing academe
which college stories had, oddly, led him to expect.
Cramped in Sauk Centre, he was rebellious in New
Haven. With the provincial sense of inferiority

which often afflicts Middle Westerners on the Atlantic seaboard, he held himself chafingly aloof, belonging to no societies, making few close friendships, prowling at night through the back quarters of the town, finding some outlet in writing sentimental verse, and reading with the voracious, self-interested zeal of a true man of letters. Socialistic, agnostic, he made what virtue he could out of his eccentricities, but he was unhappy in them. It was this which drove him away from Yale, to live, he hoped, like one of the heroes of Richard Harding Davis in Latin America, or like a conscious, intelligent proletarian nearer home. Each year, however, his vision of what he desired to be and do became more contemporary, more realistic. His experience gradually caught up with his reading and dimmed it.

Only those who knew Mr. Lewis well during the dozen years before *Main Street* can realize how much ferment and yet how much purpose coexist in him. The relative poverty which on his first trip to California limited him to fruit and bread and coffee for his diet; which educated him in the small shifts by which the city poor survive, bound to the tedious jobs which they are desperately afraid to lose; which obliged him to finish his sixth, and first successful, novel on borrowed money: this poverty never hindered him in his main career. He could be magnificent on nothing. He had the

magnificence of infinite curiosity, insatiable eager-
ness, swift, hot attractions and repulsions, perceptions like a trap, a memory like a bank, the
nervous energy of an explosion, and—what is
commonly left out of accounts of him—the industry
of a bird building a nest. He dashed through his
life as if he were a swarm, out-laughing, out-
drinking, out-assimilating almost any single man,
but the work he did was in his own individual
image. If his early novels, characteristic as they
are, were not as full-bodied as the later ones, it
was only because he was himself not yet filled, to a
lavish overflowing, with the wide and microscopic
erudition in common life which his appetite demanded. When he was filled he wrote *Main Street*.

Erudition is not so strange a term to use about
Sinclair Lewis as he himself would imagine. When
he decided to be a man of letters and not a doctor
of philosophy, scholarship lost a prodigious vessel.
He would have raged through libraries and torn
the hearts out of countless books. In ten years he
would have known ten times as much as the dry
specialists who would have done their best, and
that perhaps enough, to keep him from advance-
ment in almost any university. And his knowledge
would have been precise. He is a sergeant major for
details, though a general for campaigns. But as a
scholar he could not have lived on the close air of a
seminar. He would have had to do his chief work

in the field. Some more formal investigator might have studied the folk-ways and speech-habits of some distant primitive tribe and might have become famous as an anthropologist on a fraction of the knowledge which Mr. Lewis has gathered concerning millions of Americans. Mr. Lewis, putting his knowledge to living use, has written novels, not monographs, but he has mastered his phase of anthropology and has given the world his documents. Though he has primarily told stories, he has packed his books with the incidental substance of whole treatises about the manners of Middle Western villages and smaller towns, of men in business and in the professions, of Americans in the Canadian wilds or in bewildering European cities, of clerks, stenographers, motorists, aviators, and a multitude of human odds and ends, not one of them shown for even the length of a paragraph without some distinguishing stroke of observation. If this is not learning, the term is too narrow. There are scholars whose erudition comes from life.

Mr. Lewis has plenty of method in his acquisition of knowledge and in his employment of it, but the processes at first sight seem too rapid to be anything but instinct. He appears to be driven, rather than to drive himself. He has a flair for experts. Identifying them at a glance or at the sound of a syllable, seizing hold on them before they realize it, he squeezes out whatever they have for him, discarding, or disregarding, the rest as if it had never come to the surface. He has mountains of information, and none of it, to him, useless. If he sometimes does not see or hear, it does not matter, since he has that skin which is all eyes and ears. In spite of what is often said about him, he is not a supreme reporter. One visit to a scene, for example, is never enough for him. He may go away with scrappy images of the landscape, streets, interiors, even of the people, as he will probably go away without the methodical notes of some realistic novelists. He must return until he has been saturated—until, that is, the scene has entered into him through all the channels of assimilation. Only then will his story move, with the rush of an instinct like that with which he discovers and absorbs his materials.

It is this sensitiveness of his nerves which has made him seismographic to the ground swell of American popular thinking and feeling for a dozen years. *Main Street* was written, not merely because Mr. Lewis saw it was time to take a new attitude towards the village, or because other writers just before him had been cuffing the idol, but because he had registered in himself the stirrings of a general discontent. He was one of millions of Americans who had come to think of their villages as dull in comparison with the more variegated worlds spread before them by newspapers, motion pictures, excursions in train or automobile. He was one of thousands who had left their villages and with more distaste than homesickness remembered them in difficult but exciting towns. For all his gifts of expression, he was very near the run of the newer order of Americans in his specific resentments and his implied censures of the village. He was, of course, nearer than he guessed. *Main Street* came from an obstinate determination to tell what Mr. Lewis believed was a true story whether anybody would read it or not. It was a dubious experiment which took up twelve hours a day for what he thought might turn out to be an unprofitable year. The reception came as a surprise, the unexpected fulfillment of a prophecy by a prophet who did not know he was prophesying. In his conscious intellect Mr. Lewis was, so far as he was sociological at all, a humanitarian socialist. In his instinctive, seismographic nerves he caught few doctrinal dissatisfactions. Or, to change the metaphor, he was a loud-speaker which magnified into one dramatic voice the widespread mutterings of many isolated rebels who had not yet found out, though they learned it from *Main Street*, that they were in agreement.

Babbitt almost as truly as *Main Street* was the tracing of a seismographic needle. If Mr. Lewis had been a doctrinaire he might have made his life story of a realtor the exposure of a capitalist fattening upon unearned profits from the rise of values in land. Instead, Babbitt is judged by no economic standards more rigorous than those of a native American radicalism, without much emphasis. The concerns of this human comedy reach beyond any abstract concept. What Mr. Lewis revealed about Babbitt was what all perceptive Americans had already begun to detect in such business men: the uncertainty of their purposes, the insecurity of their fortunes, the pretensions with which they covered up their self-distrust, the adolescency in their societies and jargons and amusements, the infantilism of their imaginations. Not that even perceptive Americans were generally agreed on these points, which were still in the vague region of half-ideas, uncertain and unfocused. Mr. Lewis, sniffing the premonitory air, caught the suspicions and fixed them into beliefs. There can be no doubt that he worked with a creative force which, making Babbitt intensely dramatic, gave him an eminence as a type which was more than he as an individual deserved. Mr. Lewis had to be an artist because he was and is and always will be an artist. But the reception of the book was evidence that Mr. Lewis had once more shown himself to be a seismographic, the seismographic, American. Not all his creative force could have superimposed the figure of Babbitt upon unformed opinion if there had not been a wide-scattered readiness for this conception. Mr. Lewis, erudite and sensitive, had once more prophesied upon the testimony taken, more or less unconsciously, by his subtle nerves.

For *Elmer Gantry* there had been a definite fore-runner in H. L. Mencken, who for energetic years had gone on pointing out that the backward counties of the United States were ridden by clergymen not in the least like the gentle pastors of ordinary fiction. In a sense, Gantry is Mr. Mencken's criticism rendered in flesh and blood, put into drama, and set moving. The rough outlines of the figure had been already drawn, by Mr. Mencken and by many smaller skeptics who had read Paine and Ingersoll and Darrow and had, with the further help of their own eyes, noted flaws enough in actual ministers. What Mr. Lewis did was less to precipitate a storm that few besides him knew was gathering than to bring together, with an erudition nobody before him had matched, the materials for the most damning story of a false preacher that has ever been told in America. He did not need to be as seismographic as he had been in *Main Street* and *Babbitt*, and he was not. But he was massively and acutely learned. His learning, moreover, was as native as baseball. Not only did he choose a hero who could have belonged to no other soil, and exhibit him in a series of circum-stances which on the whole fitted him like changes of clothing, but he studied the rascal in the light of average American assumptions. The country at large might deny that it had Gantrys in it, but the village saint could agree with the village atheist that this particular Gantry, if he existed, was all that Mr. Lewis represented. He drank. He wenched. He was an obvious hypocrite. These vices stood out in the record above his ignorance, his cruelty, his meanness, his lack of imagination and spiritual perception. Though Mr. Lewis knew what Gantry's worst faults were, he felt the vices in the man which most Americans would feel, and hate. His American nerves told the story as much as his cosmopolitan intelligence.

To apply an Emersonian distinction, Mr. Lewis is not merely an American story-teller but also an American telling stories, as Mark Twain was. Mr. Lewis, however, has a mind better disciplined than Mark Twain's, and more mental and moral courage. Perhaps the later story-teller has been happier in his times. The decade just past had a whole party of opinion which realized that the United States in "going through a revolutionary change from rustic colony to world-empire" had altered "the bucolic and Puritanic simplicity of Uncle Sam," and which could give support to a novelist whose forthright patterns satisfied its understanding of the change. Mr. Lewis has owed his vogue, in part, to the thoroughness with which he summed up in himself the hopes and fears of the new age and, whether deliberately or not, challenged the old one. In his novels, more than in any others, the new age found itself, because in him, more than in any other good novelist, the new age was epitomized.

Yet the ground swell in America during the years after the war must not be credited with too large a share in Mr. Lewis's achievements. Many Americans had the same chance as he to record it. It was he alone who did. And no observer can be certain just where to draw the line between what Mr. Lewis registered and what, by giving it the form of lifelike narratives, he virtually created; be certain, that is to say, whether without *Main Street* and *Babbitt* and *Elmer Gantry* there would ever have been that body of discontent which is, after the fact, held to account for the swift prosperity of those books. Without any ground swell *Arrowsmith* and *Dodsworth* also were prosperous with their readers.

Neither of them depended upon a rising sentiment for its reception. The practice of medicine was not under fire in America. Such a career as Martin Arrowsmith's Mr. Lewis might have projected for himself, imagining, as a member of a medical family, what could have happened if he had followed the profession of brother, father, uncle, and grandfather, and had been, successively, country doctor, public health official, pathologist in a fashionable clinic, bacteriologist in an institute for medical research, commissioner sent from New York to fight a plague in the West Indies, and, in the end, hermit of science with a laboratory in Vermont. Martin's prayer transcends the general human ambition, in America or anywhere else: "God give me unclouded eyes and freedom from haste. God give me a quiet and relentless anger against all pretense and all pretentious work and all work left slack and unfinished. God give me a restlessness whereby I may neither sleep nor accept praise till my observed results equal my calculated results or in pious glee I discover and assault my error. God give me strength not to trust in God!" Although *Arrowsmith* is the most extensive and the most complete of all Mr. Lewis's chronicles, and although it does for an American profession what no other novel has ever done, it records the passion of a highly distinctive individual and measures all his society by his standards. The story had to come from within the novelist himself, or from within somebody like him in integrity, not from tremors in the social ground. The readers who responded had to admire rather than recognize. Nevertheless, they found in the story an established honorable American pattern of behavior. Arrowsmith, despairing of medicine because of its worldly confusions and short-sighted compromises, turns his back on it to do his true work in a wilderness, almost exactly as Leather-Stocking and Daniel Boone had in the eighteenth century turned away from the corrupted settlements to be themselves beyond the tumult of mankind.

Dodsworth most among Mr. Lewis's major novels follows with steady concentration the workings of a single troubled heart. "Samuel Dodsworth was, perfectly, the American Captain of Industry, believing in the Republican Party, high tariff, and, so long as they did not annoy him personally, in prohibition and the Episcopal Church. He was the president of the Revelation Motor Company; he was a millionaire, though decidedly not a multimillionaire; his large house was on Ridge Crest, the most fashionable street in Zenith; he had some taste in etchings; he did not split many infinitives; and he sometimes enjoyed Beethoven. He would certainly (so the observer assumed) produce excellent motor cars; he would make impressive speeches to the salesman; but he would never love passionately, lose tragically, nor sit in contented idleness upon tropic shores." It is these unexpected things that Dodsworth does do in the story, which takes him out of his native circumstances to give him more leisure in which to be tormented by his wife's disloyalty and desertion. His intensely personal fortune are no less intensely national. Without being stridently cocksure, like Mark Twain's innocents abroad, or blushing and colonial, like Henry James's dilettantes in Europe, Dodsworth is the essence of America on its grand tour. Himself simple, dignified, unhappy, he comes in contact with all the more extravagant varieties of his American kind. The book is a gallery of expatriates. Both in implied contrasts and in outspoken conversations the differences between America and Europe are set forth, not only with the traditional comedy and the traditional nostalgia, but with, in addition, a reasoned balancing of values which few Americans had or could have before the war. Yet Mr. Lewis in *Dodsworth* consolidated no drifting rumors, just ready to be brought into a new unity of opinion. The personal fortunes of Dodsworth are almost pure drama. He is an infatuated husband who barely saves himself from an unendurable wife. The story of Dodsworth and Fran belongs to the general history of human passion, though perhaps only Americans can be such husbands, and only Americans such wives.

Out of Mr. Lewis's five major novels *Main Street*, *Babbitt*, and *Elmer Gantry* have had the advantage of a startling timeliness and *Arrowsmith* and *Dodsworth* have got along without it. Timeliness alone can therefore not explain his power. Nor can it be explained by his art alone, skilful as that may be shown to be. The power is largely in the man and must be looked for there.

What has been overlooked by almost all his judges is his stubborn simplicity. He is not a critic taking his world apart, but a highly sensitized American telling stories. His work contains no tight scheme of doctrine, moral, social, political, or theological. Tested by any strict ideologist, he would turn out to be full of contradictions. His strain of native radicalism is a strong, humane instinct towards the side of justice, freedom, decency, kindness, but it has never amounted to a system. In his emotions he has been conditioned by common American experiences. Much as he has traveled, he remains something of the Middle Westerner, a little confused by New York, a little awed by Europe, a little suspicious before complexity and elegance though at the same time delighted with them. A satirist at home or with other Americans, he is a patriot abroad or with foreigners. Women of much intricacy he appears to rank, like many an American man, among the secrets of nature, beguiling but not entirely to be comprehended. Towards women in general he has about the attitude of masculine America when it is not wearing its conventional chivalry. That is, he tends to like and trust them, to depend reasonably upon them, and to look to men for his chief friendships and recognitions. Sentimental more often than cynical, he enjoys coming upon instances of modest courage, good sense, natural courtesy, unpretentious expertness, beauty in a corner. Such instances he frequently proclaims beyond their deserts, out of generous sentiment. He accepts praise somewhat shyly, gives it freely. Though he can now and then be suddenly pugnacious, he does not hold resentments long, and he has been heard to argue that he does not hate anybody on earth. Hating is no more his forte than loving, liking, or approving. Upon his close friends, who have had a chance to see him at ease, the impression he always makes is that of an extraordinary sweetness of nature.

This sweetness seems at times pathetic, in view of the course on which his rushing energy has driven him. He is a driven as well as a seismographic man. He must tell this or that story as another man must love this or that woman—without reason, perhaps, but also without rest. Mr. Lewis's minor writings are simply flirtations. His imagination has had but one great desire: to possess the actual America and to exhibit it in intelligible, worthy narratives. The passion of Theodore Dreiser has been to turn up with his powerful spade the neglected subsoil of American life; of H. L. Mencken, to nail the hides of a million American absurdities upon an immeasurable barndoor; of Eugene O'Neill, to reduce the most tragic complications to the language and dimensions of the American theatre; of James Branch Cabell, to throw the light of wit and beauty upon the endless comedy of disillusion; of Edwin Arlington Robinson, to study the mysteries of the heart in whatever past or present he finds hearts to study. Not one of them has kept so close to the main channel of American life as Mr. Lewis, or so near to the human surface. He is a part of channel and surface. To venture into hyperbole, not only is he an American telling stories, but he is America telling stories. Those special gifts which have made him a spokesman have allowed him to be himself to the extent of looking forward rather than backward, so that he is not, flabbily, all of America. But he is more of it than any other significant man of letters is. He can lose his place only upon some change in America to which he cannot adapt himself. Even if that takes place, he will be one of the first to see it coming. And Americans in general may have to learn from Sinclair Lewis that Sinclair Lewis is no longer the quintessence of the United States.

III. CRAFTSMAN

MOST good stories are old: that is, they conform to some familiar type, like newborn children. But to be, though old, still good, a story must, again like a newborn child, have a life of its own, its own flesh and blood and individual character. The biological simile may be carried further. When the teller of a story goes to the extent of being the writer of a novel, it means that he has fallen in love with his materials as with a woman, fixed his passion and his imagination upon them, and has, to pursue the image, begotten his book. Deriving from him in this or that degree, it derives also from its mother the materials, and from the general human substance of which the father and mother were carriers and conveyers. Still keeping the image, but not pressing it too close, important novelists are distinguished from unimportant by superiority of passion for their materials, superiority in the quantity of themselves contributed to their offspring, superiority in the quality of their contributions, measured as truth, beauty, music, laughter, or otherwise indefinable magic.

Although story-telling, in its essence, may be as much a mystery as reproduction, nevertheless a good deal is known about the embryonic processes through which masses of life pass in becoming threads of narrative. These processes can be studied in Sinclair Lewis with little difficulty. His raw materials are still fresh in the minds by which his finished products have been accepted. The impulses which have driven him to create, though profound and powerful, are simple. The forms in which he has cast his creations are intelligible, his personal biases seldom mystifying.

To begin with, he is a story-teller by nature. Perhaps this means only that, born with the energy to live stories, he has somehow been repressed or diverted by circumstances into telling them. Nobody can be sure that the story-telling faculty is ever more than a writer's second nature. But the second nature of Sinclair Lewis, if it is no more than that, has the strength of original instinct, the strength of a will to action. He gives himself to his stories as other men give themselves to their lives. His immense assimilations do not make him heavy, hesitant, inarticulate. Carrying his weight with relative ease, he goes ahead with an exciting directness and speed. He hides behind no dim abstractions, falls into no vague speculations, follows his shadow around no interminable circles. The line reaching from his first page to his last in any novel may be long but will be straight. All the tumults which he goes through, and takes others through, in deciding upon a theme, a method, a development, a conclusion; in collecting and transmuting his substances; in making false starts and drawing back from them; in wondering, doubting, temporarily despairing whether the way of his passion is the way of wisdom: all this tumult is the friction inseparable from movement. He moves constantly, and always forward, as if forces not himself were compelling him. He will, said one of his friends, write till he drops. And another friend added that it would hardly be safe to trust him with a typewriter in his grave.

In some writers the passion to tell stories is promiscuous, and almost any subject will serve. Mr. Lewis is highly selective and intensely personal in his choices. Far from being a disinterested chronicler of his heroes, he has in nearly every one of them projected some emotion of his own into imagined experience.

Our Mr. Wrenn and *The Job*, in a strict sense not autobiographical at all, in a larger sense may be regarded as autobiography in fictive disguises. Wrenn, a petty clerk in a New York office, equally a prey to loneliness and restlessness, is not the Sinclair Lewis of the New York years, but he is one of the little people with whom Mr. Lewis could not then help comparing himself, half-fearful of sinking to their dingy plane. When he shows Wrenn escaping from his routine to go to Liverpool on a cattle boat and to be embarrassed by delightful England, he hints at private secrets, like H. T. Webster in the shivering history of the Timid Soul. Una Golden in *The Job* has no such adventure as Mr. Wrenn, but she leads the dreary office life which Mr. Lewis had to hate and had to pity. Wrenn after his one interlude and Una after her sorry marriage are established, happily enough, in lives which promise to suit their dispositions. But while they lived, under whatever disguises, they were elements in the imagination of Mr. Lewis. He understood them because he contained them.

The Trail of the Hawk and *Free Air* deal with wishes and fears even closer to autobiography. Hawk Ericson, born in Minnesota, suddenly leaves college, takes to the road like a hero of Richard Harding Davis or Jack London, travels to Panama, learns aviation in California, in New York wins and marries an obsessing, bewildering girl, finds a settled existence unendurable, and breaks it up to run with her away from slavery in search of life. *Free Air* goes obviously over the route by which Mr. Lewis had traveled to Seattle, but the autobiography in it is not merely topographical. Between Milton Daggett of Schoenstrom, Minnesota, and Claire Boltwood of Brooklyn there is that gulf of different manners which had made the young Sinclair Lewis, of Sauk Centre, self-conscious in New Haven and New York. That Daggett is a mechanic, not a Yale man, widens the gulf without actually disguising it. For the rest, *Free Air* is a road to a happy ending as laid down by simple wishes. Daggett turns out to be a conquering hero in Middle Western homespun, Claire a woman in spite of all that Brooklyn is supposed to have done to her. And even after *Main Street* there was to be another novel as personal as any before it. In *Mantrap* a civilized lawyer from New York, Ralph Prescott, makes an expedition into the Canadian woods much as Mr. Lewis had done. Prescott's companion, blustering with virtue over his primitive hardihood, may come from life but does come from the disgust of Mr. Lewis at such affectations.

If *Mantrap*, after *Main Street*, seems a survival from an earlier period, it is because the novel is little more than an episode dramatizing a single emotion of the writer. Yet the later, greater novels, for all their bulk and scope, have also that core of personal emotion without which literature is likely to leave its readers unmoved, however edified. *Main Street* is, seen in personal terms, a story of what might have happened to Mr. Lewis if he had been only a part of himself and had succumbed to his Gopher Prairie. To have let himself sink into business, as he tried to do for five years in New York, might have made him almost satisfied with some such career as that he traced in *Babbitt*. *Arrowsmith* recounts a history he missed, perhaps, by not following his family's profession. *Elmer Gantry* represents that kind of monster the novelist most loathed. *Dodsworth*, profoundly personal, reaches down into a reservoir of actual experience to bring up its records of loneliness, defeat, and loss. No comment upon Mr. Lewis is more inaccurate than that which calls him a universal comic reporter. He is specialized by his own passions. He writes out of his own heart. His novels are his poems.

When, just after *Free Air*, the lightest of his novels, he wrote *Main Street*, it was not merely that with conscience and will he had set himself to work upon a larger scale. He could not have done it before if he had tried. The novel on the Village Virus which he had planned fifteen years before, while an undergraduate fretting out a summer vacation in Sauk Centre, would have been, written then, another minor novel. To be ready for *Main Street* he had had to saturate himself with American villages from one ocean to the other. His saturation at last complete, and his simple narrative devices mastered through experiment, he could pour all he was and all he knew into the story. He will always be best known as the author of *Main Street*, not because he was first known for it, but because he is still most to be known in it. It is the book of half his life.

He learned from the triumph of *Main Street* that his gifts justified and called for spacious themes, and he has since then been as faithful as Mark Twain to subjects worthy of him. Even when, as in *Babbitt* or *Dodsworth*, he has limited the visible action to a relatively short time, he has dealt with whole lives in whole settings. *The Job* had undertaken to do this, but its world had been a narrow one. *The Trail of the Hawk*, the earliest of Mr. Lewis's life stories, had used the rudiments of all his maturer methods, but had failed to be the *Arrowsmith* of flying because of something callow in its conception. Beginning with *Main Street*, his work has had no worse sign of narrowness than interest in details and no worse sign of callowness than youthfulness of spirit. His scale has been as large as his passion. Only the Mark Twain of *The Innocents Abroad, Roughing It, Life on the Mississippi, Huckleberry Finn,* and *A Connecticut Yankee in King Arthur's Court* has, among American writers, equaled in the average dimensions of his themes the Sinclair Lewis of *Main Street, Babbitt, Arrowsmith, Elmer Gantry,* and *Dodsworth.*

A powerful instinct to tell stories, a need to tell stories not too far removed from personal experience or concern, a will to tell stories of weight and range: with these impulses Mr. Lewis begins a novel. No matter how strong they may be in him, however, he will not proceed unless he can see the whole length of the way ahead. For three years he recently worked on a novel which was to be about labor in the United States. Unable to feel that he had reached saturation with his theme, he could not decide upon a plot. Unless he knew everything he could not tell anything. The American labor movement had no form. It was a chaos and a tangle of politics. In time he hit upon a plan. Baffled by the conflict of antagonisms which reached into America from Europe, he would stay native, and would tell the story of three generations of American radicals: a circuit rider of the frontier breed, a sentimental, heroic socialist, a scientific social engineer. All that was generous and expansive in Mr. Lewis grew warm at the prospect of chronicling three heroes in a row. This would be his history of a hundred American years. He read a library of books. He drew up a magnificent genealogical chart of the family of Aaron Gadd. But the story would not take a final shape in the novelist's imagination. More than half of it had run its course in a world of which he could know nothing at first hand. He might find out enough about it for a historian, but not enough for a novelist. He gave up the whole enterprise between one day and the next.

It was the lavish self-denial of a man who knew there were multitudes of novels in him. That it meant throwing away work already done and having to do more did not deter him. Almost at once he was busy with the novel to be called *Ann Vickers* and looking beyond that to another of which it is still too early to announce even the design. Mr. Lewis has always acted as if the supply of materials and labor were infinite. After giving half a lifetime to his preparations for *Main Street*, he has atoned for this unintended partiality by the most spendthrift devotion to the groundwork of his later novels. *Babbitt* is the focus of the biographies of several characters besides George Babbitt, all of which had been drawn up in detail. Zenith was built upon a map, and the plans even of houses and offices had been worked out and set down. The swarm of minor characters is managed with the apparent fortuitousness of nature because they had been thoroughly studied and could be brought into the action with deliberate, strategic, casual-seeming art. Having their places in the imagined city, and being fully imagined in their own right, they take their places in the novel without awkwardness, like men and women encountered in actual affairs. And in *Arrowsmith*, *Elmer Gantry*, *Dodsworth*, which employ an easy arrangement nearer chronicle than drama, there is the same effect: the wealth of life displayed seems to be only a part of a vast whole pressing toward the scene and likely at any moment to burst in upon it. For the village of *Main Street*, the town of *Babbitt*, the European panorama of *Dodsworth*, Mr. Lewis could draw from his own experiences. In *Arrowsmith* he had to become familiar with the career of a physician, and in *Elmer Gantry* with that of a clergyman, on a scale of equal minuteness. In the company of first one expert and then another he plunged into these careers as into jungles and came out of each with what was, even to his demands, an exact survey of the terrain and a mastery of the fauna and flora native to it. If it were necessary to do more work for this or that novel than for some other, Mr. Lewis would, as always, do more work. His eventual power over his materials must be, so far as he can manage it, complete.

A passion for his materials may make a novelist prolix and tedious, like a father so intensely interested in his child as to be excessively communicative about it. Mr. Lewis's novels are long, and full of details gathered with a tireless passion. But they are never tedious, for the reason that he commands his theme as truly as he desires it. Once under way, his countless preparations settled, he moves through the narrative with a rush which keeps it warm and nervous. His methods are as simple as improvisation looks to be. Being essentially the life story of a single person, every novel closely follows a biographical thread, seldom burdened by subsidiary plots, and employing incidents, situations, additional characters to increase the light which falls on the protagonist. Clearly as the many additional characters may be conceived, painstakingly as they may be executed, they are all subordinate. Reading the stories of Carol Kennicott, Babbitt, Arrowsmith, Elmer Gantry, and Dodsworth is like intimately accompanying them and, by the rules of a strict plot, meeting only those acquaintances and situations that they would meet. It is also, however, understanding those incidents and persons as well as Sinclair Lewis understands them. The intimate spectator reviews the varied field.

Such command as Mr. Lewis has over his material ought to have made it generally realized that he is less reporter or compiler or arranger than creator. If James Branch Cabell has created and populated the medieval French county of Poictesme, Mr. Lewis has created the contemporary Middle Western state of Winnemac, impossibly "bounded by Michigan, Ohio, Illinois, and Indiana," and more or less dominated by its principal city of Zenith, where most of the roads of the novels—except in *Main Street*—sooner or later cross. Babbitt there runs through his little year of discontent and turns back to grace. Arrowsmith, studying medicine at the university a few miles away, finds Leora at a Zenith hospital. Elmer Gantry hitches his clattering wagon to the star of Zenith. Dodsworth, when his peace has been broken and healed in Europe, still thinks of Zenith as his home. Side by side with actual Middle Western cities, hardly to be distinguished one from the other except by name, Zenith has appeared to be pure nature. But Zenith is art. When the actual cities have faded into history, Zenith, with all its garish colors and comic angles, will stand up like a living monument. It will be the hub of the universe which Mr. Lewis has shaped out of the Middle West of his age. Already his version of this Zenith-centered world has supplanted the versions of most novelists before him. Distant strangers know the Middle West as Zenith, with villages and towns like Gopher Prairie and Wheatsylvania and Nautilus and Babylon and Banjo Crossing as its scattered, sprawling neighbors. Even in the Middle West men and women have had to look twice at their own faces in the mirror to be sure that they are or are not like the men and women of Zenith and its suburbs. There have been bitter arguments as to whether Mr. Lewis has told the truth about his native land, or how much of the truth, or with what passion or dispassion.

These are vain arguments. Mr. Lewis has all

along been telling the life stories of particular persons who have laid hold on his imagination. Because it is his nature to assimilate whatever touches him, and to be extraordinarily erudite in all his records, he has the opulence which is too easily confused with mere transcription of human life. But he has also the exuberance which, more than any other quality, distinguishes the commanding realist from his drudging rivals. All the characters, actions, situations, incidents, conversations in his novels are edged and heightened. The pitiless monologue of Lowell Schmaltz, in *The Man Who Knew Coolidge*, is a leaden treasury which future scholars will mine for twentieth-century platitudes, but Schmaltz is not allowed to be a mere flat-footed bore. He is put through tremendous paces of monotony by his creator, who with evident delight sees commonplace follow commonplace out of the smug mouth in an inexhaustible series. Something like this creative delight touches a great deal of the dialogue in all the novels. The speakers are, again and again, more inflated, more affected, more sentimental, more slangy, more vulgar, more ridiculous than life, much as the speakers in a play are more terse and logical, and the speakers in a poem more poetical. The whole tone of Mr. Lewis's novels is raised above the level of bald realism by the dialogue, which owes its satisfying sound to his mimetic gift and its lasting force to his imperious energy. His narrative has to be swift and exuberant to keep up with his dialogue.

Important novelists are distinguished from unimportant by superiority of passion for their materials, superiority in the quantity of themselves contributed, superiority in the quality of their contributions, measured as truth, beauty, music, laughter, or otherwise indefinable magic. As to the passion with which Mr. Lewis has given all of himself to his novels there is not much doubt. The critical debate which has most steadily persisted concerns the quality of his creations. Where, it is often asked, are the large issues which rule his world? The answer is that they are in his books. The desire of Carol Kennicott is for beauty, of Babbitt for freedom, of Arrowsmith for integrity in the pursuit of knowledge, of Gantry for ruthless power, of Dodsworth for loyalty in love. That only Arrowsmith among them follows his desire to some ultimate conclusion need not obscure the fact that the issues are all large, and that Mr. Lewis knows they are. In this knowledge, and in the conviction sprung from it, he firmly guides his heroes to their ends. But, with a passion for life more intense and more faithful than any moralist's can be, he takes his characters the size he finds them, and cuts their issues to fit their natures. Even Arrowsmith is not a Faust, the intellectual and moral heir of accumulated centuries. He is a Middle Western bacteriologist, half-taught except in his specialty, little more than a stubborn artisan in the great world of human thought. Arrowsmith the symbol barely shows itself behind Arrowsmith the fact. And so with Mr. Lewis's characters in general. Behind them or beyond them there may be as great a cosmos as any philosopher can imagine or construct. Mr. Lewis himself has looked into it with his restless eyes. It does not feed his hunger. His universe is at his feet, around his head. Pity and terror rise in him at trifles which cosmic novelists might overlook. When he wants to indicate that Dodsworth, deserted by his wife, stranded in Paris, is as lonely as a star lost outside the thinnest fringes of infinite space, where nothing binds him any longer to others or to himself and he faints under an excess of time which he has lost the power to use or kill, Mr. Lewis packs all his meaning into one dry tragicomic sentence. "He never admitted it to himself, but he neglected giving a hotel address to the Guaranty Trust, so that he might have a reason to plod to the bank for his mail every day." The fact is here the symbol, and any elaboration of the symbol a superfluous impertinence.

If the truth of these novels must be sought for in the facts, and found there only, so must their beauty. They have bold design and sure proportions, and the color and movement of vitality. But, being of the same material throughout, they have no surface of plating. The style is the story, the story's well paved road, the story's rapid vehicle. It runs but does not fly. It is precise but not exquisite, sensitive but not fastidious, direct but seldom breath-taking, rich in its fullness not in its adornment. Its best music is plain-song, without complicating harmony. "When a man straggles on the short death-walk from his cell through the little green door, into the room where stands the supreme throne, does he, along with his incredulous apprehension, along with trying to believe that this so-living and eternal-seeming center and purpose of the universe, himself—this solid body with its hard biceps, its curiously throbbing heart that ever since his mother's first worry has in its agonies been so absorbing, this red-brown skin that has glowed after the salt sea at Coney Island and has turned a sullen brick after wild drinking—the astonishment that this image of God and Eternity will in five minutes be still and stiff and muck— is he at that long slow moment nonetheless conscious of a mosquito bite, of a toothache, of the smugness of the messages from Almighty God which the chaplain gives him, of the dampness of the slimy stone corridor and the echo of their solemn march?" Usually, however, the style is content to find its prose way between two points and go quickly on to another.

65

The poetry of this style appears almost wholly as exuberance. Above the essential irony of the actions there is a continuous play of laughter, pointing at whatever calls for ridicule or sympathy. The exuberance which crowds the story with so much true matter accompanies it to be sure that nothing is missed. Such integrity as Sinclair Lewis's without his exuberance might be too bitter, such exuberance without his integrity, too sweet. He displays them both in a convincing, appealing, amusing compound which, in some manner beyond analysis, brews his special magic.

Perhaps magic is not quite the term to use about a novelist who depends less upon ingratiating refinements in his art than upon force and sinew. There is, however, a masculine kind of magic, or power, and it has marked the course of fiction from Fielding, through Smollett, Scott, Dickens, Mark Twain, to Sinclair Lewis, as truly as the feminine kind has marked it from Richardson, through Jane Austen, the Brontës, Henry James, George Moore, to John Galsworthy. The two lines are of course not altogether parallel or separate, and they are not determined by the mere sex of the writers. Thackeray belongs partly to both lines, and George Eliot. But the main distinction holds. The novels with a feminine quality have something which outwardly corresponds to that subcutaneous tissue which gives to a woman's body the soft and rounded grace which a man's does not have. Though this quality appears in the texture of the prose, it goes deeper, to the themes selected, the attitudes taken, the perceptions and intuitions and implications. Beside them the novels with a masculine quality may seem to be hard, rough, careless, even obtuse, trusting to strength before subtlety, and running over delicate obstacles as if they did not exist. No novelist in English has perfectly combined both qualities, employing the hand of Dickens in the glove of Henry James. Mr. Lewis, who belongs clearly in the masculine line, is not to be estimated with too much reference to the other. In an age when the distinguished novelists of his language tend to be, as the term is here used, feminine, he has kept to the line which, if the two lines must be weighed, must be seen to be the greater. Sinclair Lewis will outlast John Galsworthy.

CHRONOLOGY

CHRONOLOGY

1885: 7 February, Sinclair Lewis born at Sauk
Centre, Minnesota. Son of Dr. Edwin J.
Lewis (son of John Lewis and Emeline Johnson
Lewis) and Emma Kermott Lewis (daughter
of Dr. Edward Payson Kermott and Elizabeth
Plews Kermott). Two brothers. (Mother died
1890. Father subsequently married Isabel
Warner.)

1890–1902: Attended elementary and high schools
in Sauk Centre and studied Greek with the
Episcopal minister. Engaged in usual sports.
Read widely and irregularly.

1902–03: Six months at Oberlin Academy, Oberlin,
Ohio, preparing for Yale.

1903–06: Student at Yale College. Most interested
in English, rhetoric, psychology, economics.
Continued to read enormously and planlessly.
Wrote for the Yale *Literary Magazine* (one of
its editors) and *Courant.* During the summer
vacations of 1904 and 1906 to England on

cattleboats. During the summer of 1905 at Sauk Centre working on a novel to be called *The Village Virus* (unfinished, but the first study for *Main Street*).

1906: Bored with Yale, spent October-November at Helicon Hall, Englewood, New Jersey, acting as janitor, along with Allan Updegraff (Yale friend).

1906–07: Lived as a free lance in New York with Allan Updegraff, in the Gashouse district of Avenue B and in the Bronx. Worked in a department store during the Christmas rush. Wrote sentimental verses for children. From March, 1907, to October, assistant editor of *Transatlantic Tales*, translating from French and German. October, went to Panama, traveling steerage and failing to find a job there.

1907–08: Back at Yale to complete the work for his degree in June, 1908. Enough pleased with academic life to think of taking a Ph. D. in English.

1908–10: Spent two years as a wandering free lance with occasional employment. During the summer of 1908 did editorial jobs for eight weeks on the *Courier* at Waterloo, Iowa. In the fall, to New York, to work for the Joint Application Bureau of the Charity Organization Society and the Association for the Improvement of the Condition of the Poor.

Having sold a story to the *Red Book*, for $75, left New York in a day coach for California, to serve as part-time secretary for six or seven months to Alice Macgowan and Grace Macgowan Cooke (formerly of Helicon Hall) at Carmel. In his spare time wrote constantly, and sold one joke to *Judge*. Shared a cottage with William Rose Benét (Yale friend) at Carmel and visited Benét's family at Benicia. For three months a reporter on the San Francisco *Bulletin*, edited by Fremont Older. For another three months, wire editor for the Associated Press in San Francisco. Dismissed from both posts for incompetence. To Washington, D. C., to assist F. K. Noyes (Yale friend), editor of the *Volta Review* for teachers of the deaf.

1910–15: For five years, occupied with various phases of publishing. Two years as manuscript reader for Frederick A. Stokes. Assistant editor of *Adventure* magazine. Editor and chief reviewer of the Publishers' Newspaper Syndicate, organized by W. E. Woodward to furnish a syndicated book-review page for newspapers. Editor and advertising manager for George H. Doran. April, 1914, married Grace Livingstone Hegger of New York. December, 1915, having sold stories to *Saturday Evening Post*, resigned from Doran and publishing.

1914: Our Mr. Wrenn published.

1915: The Trail of the Hawk published.

1915–20: Five years, again a wandering free lance supported by short stories and serials for magazines. Winter of 1915–16 at St. Augustine, Florida. Summer of 1916 to Chicago, to Sauk Centre, and by motor via Duluth, Miles City, Yellowstone Park, Seattle, San Francisco, to Carmel. By train to the Grand Canyon and to New Orleans, by steamer to New York. Son, Wells, born in New York August, 1917. Winter of 1917–18 at St. Paul, Minnesota. Summer of 1918 on Cape Cod. Winter of 1918–19 at Minneapolis. Summer of 1919 at Mankato, Minnesota. In Minnesota revised and completed plans for *Main Street*, written in Washington, D. C., during 1919–20.

1917: The Job published.

The Innocents published.

1919: Free Air published.

Hobohemia (play) produced in New York.

1920: Main Street published.

1921–22: Early in 1921 went lecturing and disliked it. In May to Europe, to write *Babbitt* in Cornwall, Kent, at Lago Maggiore, Rome, London. Summer of 1922 to Sauk Centre. Took a house in Hartford, Connecticut, but soon gave it up.

1922: Babbitt published.

1922–25: With Paul De Kruif inspected laboratories in New York and Washington, and went on a small steamer to the Lesser Antilles, Venezuela, Panama, and London, studying tropic medicine and working on the plan of *Arrowsmith*. Wrote the novel in France, near Fontainebleau, summer of 1923. Revised it in London, winter–spring of 1923–24. To America spring, 1924. With brother, Dr. Claude Lewis, to northern Saskatchewan and Manitoba, along the Churchill River, summer of 1924. Fall of 1924 to late spring of 1925 in London, Paris, southern France, Italy, Bavaria, Austria, Berlin. Summer of 1925 in Westchester County, writing *Mantrap*.

1925: Arrowsmith published.

1926–27: After visit to California and Arizona spent winter of 1925–26 in Kansas City studying the habits of the Middle Western clergy, with the assistance of the Rev. L. M. Birkhead. May, refused the Pulitzer award to *Arrowsmith*. Summer of 1926 with the Birkheads on a lake in northern Minnesota, writing *Elmer Gantry*, completed in Washington, D. C. winter of 1926–27. Dr. Edwin J. Lewis died 1926.

1926: Mantrap published.

1927–28: February, 1927, to Europe, wandering alone. To Paris, Venice, Corfu, Athens, Vienna. With Ramon Guthrie on a walking trip in

Alsace and the Schwartzwald. From Berlin in July flew to Vienna with Dorothy Thompson, representing the New York *Evening Post* and Philadelphia *Public Ledger* in Central Europe, to cover Viennese revolution. July, 1927, to May, 1928, in Berlin, Cornwall, London, Naples, writing *The Man Who Knew Coolidge* and part of *Dodsworth*. Divorced from Grace Hegger Lewis, April, 1928, and married Dorothy Thompson next month. Spent the summer of 1928 touring England in a motor caravan. Returned to America in the fall and bought a farm at Barnard, Vermont, where *Dodsworth* was completed.

1927: Elmer Gantry published.

1928: The Man Who Knew Coolidge published.

1929: Dodsworth published.

1929–32: Spent the summers of 1929, 1930, 1931, 1932 at Barnard, the winters of 1928–29, 1929–30, 1931–32 in New York, the winter of 1930–31 at Westport, Connecticut. Second son, Michael, born August, 1930. Awarded the Nobel Prize in December, 1930, went to Stockholm and spent Christmas in Berlin. November, 1931, to August, 1932, wrote *Ann Vickers* in New York and Barnard. In August left America for indefinite stay in villa at Semmering, Austria.

1933: Ann Vickers published.

BIBLIOGRAPHY
OF THE
WRITINGS
OF
SINCLAIR LEWIS
BY
HARVEY TAYLOR

CONTENTS

	PAGE
FOREWORD	81
CHRONOLOGICAL LIST OF BOOKS BY SINCLAIR LEWIS	85
CHRONOLOGICAL LIST OF CONTRIBUTIONS TO BOOKS	87
BOOKS BY SINCLAIR LEWIS; FIRST EDITIONS COLLATED	91
CONTRIBUTIONS TO BOOKS; FIRST EDITIONS DESCRIBED	129
CONTRIBUTIONS TO PERIODICALS: 1903–1932	147
SELECTED BIOGRAPHICAL AND CRITICAL NOTICES IN BOOKS	175
SELECTED BIOGRAPHICAL AND CRITICAL NOTICES IN PERIODICALS	181
HARPER & BROTHERS' CODE	185
NOTES	187
INDEX TO THE BIBLIOGRAPHY	193

FOREWORD

It is due time for a bibliography of the writings of Sinclair Lewis to be published. For years collectors of Lewis first editions have depended upon not always accurate or complete guides, or the advice of book dealers in whom they have confidence. There has been no certainty as to the Harper's Code letters in relation to the Lewis books, or data on the first issues of *Babbitt* and *Main Street* or of the value of the large-paper *Arrowsmith*. It has not been the fault of the compilers of check lists, nor should the bookmen be held responsible for any inaccuracies. Both groups have been waiting for a bibliography. Several students of Lewis's writings have announced intentions of compiling such a book, but, I found, none had gone farther than to see that various announcements had been printed.

My preparation for this list had its beginning several years ago; since that time I have been in constant contact with the Lewis first editions, collecting several sets of my own, inspecting publishers' file copies, comparing copies in many private libraries, and even going so far as to act as secretary to Mr. Lewis for a short time. In compiling the list of uncollected writings research was done in the libraries of the University of California, Stanford University Library, Yale Library, and city libraries including New York Public Library. Too, Sinclair Lewis's business files, his clipping books, and his memory have contributed well to the list of contributions to periodicals in the rear of the volume. I am indebted to Mr. Lewis, Mr. Merle Johnson, Mr. Donald C. Brace.

If a study of the American authors the first editions of whose writings are in demand were to be made the student would very readily find that these writers were appreciated abroad before America took serious interest. The names of Poe, Herman Melville, Walt Whitman, Bret Harte, Mark Twain, and Stephen Crane would fall easily into the list. I have found it interesting to note the increasing interest in Sinclair Lewis as a collected author since the award of the Nobel Prize in 1930. Immediately collectors sought *Hike and the Aëroplane*, Lewis's first book.

To compile a bibliography of an author who was once a newspaper man is a difficult task; to avoid further work in searching files I list here the further writings of Mr. Lewis for those who wish to carry their interests beyond the items listed in the book.

1898–03. Wrote personals, news of visitors, and minor social notes for Sauk Centre *Herald* and Sauk Centre *Avalanche*, often composing while setting type.

1903–08. Reporter on New Haven *Journal and Courier* while at Yale University.

1908. Reporter on Waterloo (Iowa) *Courier* for seven weeks of midsummer.

1909. Reporter on San Francisco *Bulletin* late in year.

1913–14. Editor of Publishers' Newspaper Syndicate, writing book reviews under names of Tom Graham and Sinclair Lewis for copy which appeared in the Baltimore *News*, Minneapolis *Journal*, St. Louis *Republic*, a Detroit paper, and a Pittsburgh paper.

If the student wishes to go further in his search of obscure details he might investigate the volumes of Jack London's short stories which appeared after 1911. Sinclair Lewis contributed the outlines of nine of these stories, "but," says Mr. Lewis, "neither I nor anyone else will ever be able to give definite data, because there is no filing cabinet." Someone has said, however, that all one need do in a case of literary controversy is to turn it over to a real book collector. This I do.

The forthcoming books of interest to collectors of Sinclair Lewis's first editions are: (1) Sinclair

Lewis: A Critical Essay by James Branch Cabell, with a Foreword by Harvey Taylor. (2) The Ghosts of Jack London: George Sterling and Sinclair Lewis, containing the "Lost" Stories by Lewis. Edited by Harvey Taylor. (3) Sinclair Lewis on Literary Awards. Privately issued.

The bibliographer would appreciate corrections and additions for a revised edition of his compilation.

HARVEY TAYLOR

CHRONOLOGICAL LIST OF BOOKS BY SINCLAIR LEWIS

HIKE AND THE AEROPLANE	1912
OUR MR. WRENN	1914
THE TRAIL OF THE HAWK	1915
THE JOB	1917
THE INNOCENTS	1917
FREE AIR	1919
MAIN STREET	1920
BABBITT	1922
ARROWSMITH	1925
ARROWSMITH. TRADE EDITION	1925
MANTRAP	1926
REVIEW OF "MANHATTAN TRANSFER"	1926
ELMER GANTRY	1927
THE MAN WHO KNEW COOLIDGE	1928
DODSWORTH	1929
CHEAP AND CONTENTED LABOR	1929
NOBEL PRIZE ADDRESS	1931
NOBEL PRIZE ADDRESS. REVISED EDITION	1931
NOBEL PRIZE ADDRESS. SEPARATE.	1931

SINCLAIR LEWIS

LETTER TO CRITICS   1931
SINCLAIR LEWIS ON THE VALLEY OF THE
     MOON   1932
LAUNCELOT   1932

CHRONOLOGICAL LIST OF SINCLAIR LEWIS'S CONTRIBUTIONS TO BOOKS

John Ames Mitchell   1912
History of the Class of 1907; Yale
    College   1913
Irvin Cobb: His Book   1915
Hugh Walpole   1915
The Best Short Stories of 1918   1918
"Jurgen" and the Censor   1920
My Maiden Effort   1921
These United States; Second Series   1924
Short Stories   1925
Four Days on the Webutuck River   1925
On Parade   1929
Literary Treasures of 1929   1929
The 1930 American Scrapbook   1930
The O-SA-GE, 1931   1931
Vermont Prose   1931
Opinions on Book Collecting   1931

BOOKS BY SINCLAIR LEWIS

I

(1912)

HIKE AND THE / AEROPLANE / BY / TOM
GRAHAM / WITH ILLUSTRATIONS IN TWO
COLORS BY / ARTHUR HUTCHINS / [*aero-
plane decoration*] / NEW YORK / FREDERICK
A. STOKES COMPANY / PUBLISHERS

Cr. 8vo [$7\frac{5}{16} \times 4\frac{15}{16}$].

COLLATION: Half-title, blank, blank, frontispiece
showing rescue at sea by an aëroplane titled
"*The Waves Were Increasing—The Yacht Could
Not Last Much Longer Page 51*", protection sheet,
title as above, copyright (Copyright, 1912, by /
Frederick A. Stokes Company / [*short rule*] / All
rights reserved, including that of translation into
foreign / languages, including the Scandinavian)
and publishers' emblem at left of rectangle in
lower left of page inclosing "August, 1912", dedication (To / Edwin and Isabel Lewis, / The
Author's Oldest Friends), blank, Contents, conclusion of Contents, List of Illustrations, blank,
division title, blank, text pp. 1–275, verso blank.

BINDING: Gray cloth, lettered in dark blue. Decoration on front cover stamped in dark blue, orange, and dark gray. The decoration is from the plate of the frontispiece.

FRONT COVER: (HIKE AND THE / AERO-PLANE / [*decoration same as frontispiece but without detail*] / TOM GRAHAM)

SPINE: (HIKE / AND THE / AEROPLANE / [*orange rule*] / TOM / GRAHAM / [*bird decoration*] / [*orange rule*] / STOKES)

Full-page illustrations appear as follows: frontispiece, opposite pp. 78, 148, 272.

THIS novel for boys was written in seven weeks. Lewis's opinion of it is that "it's pretty terrible, but fortunately, for the bibliographer's sake, there are a few copies in existence." The author's own copy is inscribed as follows: "To Sinclair Lewis from the author, Tom Graham, his altered ego."

Of the one thousand copies printed less than eight hundred were sold.

The author states that this novel will never be reprinted.

I I

(1914)

OUR MR. WRENN / THE ROMANTIC AD-
VENTURES / OF A GENTLE MAN / BY /
SINCLAIR LEWIS / [*publishers' seal*] / HARPER
& BROTHERS PUBLISHERS / NEW YORK
AND LONDON / MCMXIV

Cr. 8vo ($7\frac{1}{4} \times 4\frac{7}{8}$).

COLLATION: Two blank leaves, blank, frontispiece, protection sheet, title as above, copyright
(Published February, 1914 / M–N), dedication
To Grace Livingston Hegger, blank, Contents,
blank, division title, blank, text pp. 1–[253], blank
leaf.

All edges are cut.

THE first dust wrapper is printed on both sides.
The front inside flap contains an advertisement
of *Harper's Magazine*.

To November 5, 1930, Harcourt, Brace & Company had sold 13,671 copies of their reprinting.
The Harper & Brothers edition sold close to 9,500
copies.

III

(1915)

THE TRAIL OF / THE HAWK / A COMEDY / OF THE SERIOUSNESS / OF LIFE / BY / SINCLAIR LEWIS / AUTHOR OF / Our Mr. Wrenn / [*publishers' seal*] / HARPER & BROTHERS PUBLISHERS / NEW YORK AND LONDON

Title enclosed in double-line border.

Cr. 8vo ($7\frac{5}{16} \times 5$).

COLLATION: Half-title, blank, blank, frontispiece, protection sheet, title as above, copyright (Published September, 1915 / H–P), dedication of six lines, blank, division title, blank, text pp. 3–[409], blank.

BINDING: Blue cloth, stamped in gilt.

THE first dust wrapper has printing on both sides; the inside front flap contains an advertisement of *Harper's Magazine*.

In the Harcourt, Brace reprinting 10,227 copies

were sold up to November 5, 1930. Nearly 11,000 were sold in the Harper edition.

Harper & Brothers inserted in review copies of *The Trail of the Hawk* a typewritten note containing biographical material and the following quotation from an autobiographical letter from Lewis:

"I've been a hotel clerk in college vacation time; worked as a janitor at Helicon Hall, the colony which Upton Sinclair started; I twice made cattle-boat trips from Portland to Liverpool, and like Mr. Wrenn, in *Our Mr. Wrenn*, I slept in a hayloft. In 1907 I wandered down to Panama, steerage and returned stowaway. No, I haven't any advice for young authors—except myself. No, I haven't any method of writing . . . who the deuce ever had any 'method of writing' after turning out newspaper copy for ten years?"

It is likely that portions of this letter were published with a review of *The Trail of the Hawk*.

IV

(1917)

THE JOB / AN AMERICAN NOVEL / BY / SINCLAIR LEWIS / Author of / "The Trail of the Hawk" / "Our Mr. Wrenn" / [*publishers' seal*] / HARPER & BROTHERS PUBLISHERS / NEW YORK AND LONDON

Title in single-line border inclosing three panels; upper panel contains title, central panel contains author's name and two books, and the lower panel contains publishers' data.

Cr. 8vo ($7\frac{15}{16} \times 4\frac{5}{16}$).

COLLATION: Half-title, list of three Books by Sinclair Lewis, title as above, copyright (The Job / [*short rule*] / Copyright, 1917, by / Harper & Brothers / Printed in the United States of America / Published February, 1917 / B–R), dedication of six lines, blank, Contents, blank, division title, blank, text pp. 3–[327], blank verso.

BINDING: Olive-green cloth, stamped in gilt. Front cover: (The Job / Sinclair Lewis /) against gilt rectangle with gilt rules above and below.

SPINE: (The / Job / [*two short rules*] / Sinclair / Lewis / Harpers /).

IN THE Harcourt, Brace reprinting 15,276 copies were sold up to November 5, 1930. The original Harper printing sold close to 10,000 copies.

V

(1917)

THE / INNOCENTS / A STORY FOR LOVERS
/ BY / SINCLAIR LEWIS / Author of "The
Trail of the Hawk" / "The Job" Etc. / [*publishers'
seal*] / HARPER & BROTHERS PUBLISHERS
/ NEW YORK AND LONDON

Cr. 8vo. ($7\frac{3}{8} \times 4\frac{13}{16}$).

COLLATION: Half-title, list of five Books by
Sinclair Lewis, blank, frontispiece, title as above,
copyright (Published October, 1917 / F–R), A
Dedicatory Introduction, blank, text pp. 1–[217],
blank.

BINDING: light gray cloth, stamped in gilt.

THE first dust wrapper contains an advertisement
of *Harper's Magazine* on the front flap.

VI

(1919)

FREE AIR / BY / SINCLAIR LEWIS / Author
of "The Job," Etc. / [*publishers' seal*] / NEW
YORK / HARCOURT, BRACE AND HOWE /
1919

Cr. 8vo ($7\frac{5}{16} \times 5$).

COLLATION: blank leaf, title as above, copyright
of two lines and three-line printers' notice, Contents, conclusion of contents, division sheet, blank,
text pp. 3–370.

BINDING: blue cloth, title blind in decoration
on front cover, and author's name stamped be-
neath decoration.
Spine has pine tree in landscape decoration
dividing title and author, with publishers' imprint
at base.

THE first dust wrapper has a landscape scene with
motor car in lower right corner. It is printed in
yellow, green, gray, and white.
On November 5, 1930, Harcourt, Brace had sold
47,466 copies.

VII

(1920)

MAIN STREET / THE STORY OF CAROL
KENNICOTT / BY / SINCLAIR LEWIS / [*publishers' seal*] / NEW YORK / HARCOURT,
BRACE AND HOWE / 1920 /.

Cr. 8vo (7⅜ × 5).

COLLATION: Blank leaf, half-title, list of five
Novels by Sinclair Lewis, title as above, copyright
(dated 1920), dedication to James Branch Cabell
and Joseph Hergesheimer, blank, text pp. 1–451,
blank, blank leaf.

BINDING: Blue cloth, stamped in orange.

FIRST ISSUE: The first copies issued show the "y"
in "may" last line page 387 perfect; in later copies
the letter has the appearance of a "v." The "4"
in the page number bottom of page "54" is perfect
also in the early copies; later it is broken. These

typographical points are not always found in the dusty medium blue cloth; I have seen several copies with perfect sheets in light and in dark blue. Mr. Lewis's own copy is in dark blue; the publishers' copy is in the dusty medium blue; both have perfect type.

The first printing consisted of 10,000 copies.

The first dust wrapper has a scene from the main street of a small city on the front cover. It is in blue, brown, white, and cream.

On November 5, 1930, Harcourt, Brace Company had sold 538,473 copies; the reprint edition had sold above 185,000 copies.

VIII

(1922)

BABBITT / BY / SINCLAIR LEWIS / Author of "Main Street" / [*publishers' seal*] / NEW YORK / HARCOURT, BRACE AND COMPANY /.

Cr. 8vo ($7\frac{3}{8} \times 5$).

COLLATION: Blank leaf, half-title, list of six Novels by Sinclair Lewis, title as above, copyright (dated 1922), dedication To Edith Wharton, blank, text pp. 1–401, verso blank, advertisement division title, verso begins list with Sinclair Lewis first, followed by four pages of other lists.

Issued in blue cloth, stamped in orange.

THE first issue reads "to want to ruin my fellow human," page 49, fifth line from top, altered later to read "to want to ruin any fellow human,". Line four, page 49 has "Purdy" for "Lyte."

Harcourt, Brace had sold 287,505 copies to November 5, 1930.

BIBLIOGRAPHY

Although it was believed that only a few copies
of the first issue were in existence, several copies
have been uncovered since the announcement of
the points by Mr. Jake Blanck of the Merle Johnson Studios. Since this is undoubtedly the most
outstanding and influential of Mr. Lewis's novels,
it is certain to become a collectors' prize. It is
generally believed that the Nobel Prize was
awarded because of the influence of this book.

The English edition of *Babbitt* contains an Introduction by Hugh Walpole, and a Glossary. Although Sinclair Lewis has attempted to suppress
the Glossary, it seems to have appeared in all
reprints. It is contained in the Nobel Prize Edition
issued by the English publisher.

A recent French edition contains the following
Preface by Paul Morand:

"Like Babbitt, Sinclair Lewis finds the Middle
West frightful, but he does not know how to dis-
pense with it. He cannot live with it and he cannot
live without it. To all the palazzi and châteaux
of Europe he prefers a little bungalow on the
flowery heights of Zenith, where, however, no
flowers grow. He does not live on the Riviera like
Edith Wharton. He does not become a naturalized
Englishman like Henry James. He does not go
bathing in the Mediterranean with Jean Cocteau
like Glenway Wescott. It was high time for us to

discover this writer who really loves his native soil. Between two generations of cosmopolitan Americans so near, indeed too near, to ourselves, Lewis remains standing at the head of a group of men about forty-five years old, a member of what might be called the Center Party, a follower of the school of Mencken, who founded the *American Mercury* shortly after the war as a reaction against European influence. He is a citizen of a new country and wants to be sufficient to himself. The Monroe Doctrine is being extended to include the conquest of literature.

"*Dodsworth* is an exception in the work of Lewis. 'I shall never write another novel in a European setting,' he wrote to me a short time ago. He feels that it is not playing the game to go outside the limits of his country for a solution of the problems that are threatening not only the soul of the upper class but the soul of the entire nation. Sinclair Lewis is no deserter. He is staying at home to help America win her final liberties.

"Post-war America is becoming more human. It is thirsty for religious tolerance, moral freedom, sexual frankness, diffusion of the arts, and respect for the other fellow. It no longer aspires to be the world's biggest, but the world's best. It is seeking to find a balance between the necessary constraints of society and the rise of the individual. Sinclair Lewis is aiding with all his strength and his characters do likewise but fail. Babbitt is broken; he is a modest business man, not big enough to struggle against the sacred institutions to which the American has sold his soul in order to enjoy peace and prosperity. His defeat, which is described with the power, the admirable good sense and humor of a great writer, is the defeat of a whole people. That is why the book has produced such a profound upheaval in America and why it has enjoyed such a lasting success. This is the spirit in which we should read it if we wish to understand it and to be moved by what it has to say."

IX

(1925)

ARROWSMITH [*in red*] / By / SINCLAIR
LEWIS / Author of Main Street, Babbitt, etc. /
[*publishers' ornament in red*] / NEW YORK /
HARCOURT, BRACE AND COMPANY

Demy 8vo.

COLLATION: Blank page, list of seven Novels
by Sinclair Lewis, colophon signed by Sinclair
Lewis, title as above, copyright ("Copyright, 1925,
By / Harcourt, Brace and Company, Inc. / Copyright, 1924, 1925, by / The Designer Publishing
Company, Inc.) and three-line printers' notice,
note by Sinclair Lewis, blank, text pp. 1–448,
blank leaf.

BINDING: Light blue boards, with buckram spine.
Paper label on spine.

THE colophon states that this first edition consists
of 500 copies on hand-made paper, numbered and
signed by the author.

BIBLIOGRAPHY

This is the first edition, printed months before the first trade edition. The limited edition was printed in 1924; the printing bill was received by the publisher December 1, 1924. The trade edition was printed later; the bill for this printing was received February 1, 1925.

X

(1925)

FIRST TRADE EDITION

ARROWSMITH / By / SINCLAIR LEWIS /
Author of Main Street, Babbitt, etc. / [*publishers'*
ornament] / NEW YORK / HARCOURT, BRACE
AND COMPANY

Cr. 8vo.

COLLATION: Blank, list of seven Novels by Sinclair Lewis, title as above, copyright noting that
the first edition consists of 500 copies on hand-
made paper, numbered and signed by the author,
and that this is the first trade edition, note by
Sinclair Lewis, blank, text pp. 1-448, blank leaf.

BINDING: Blue cloth, stamped in orange.
Published March 5, 1925.

THERE was an issue to the book trade sent in advance of publication; it contains the first 26 pp.

108

of text, followed by 32 order blanks, and the remainder in blank leaves. It is in the same binding as the first trade edition.

203,491 copies were sold up to November 5, 1930.

Because Arrowsmith is the name used by an English publishing house, the title was altered to *Martin Arrowsmith* for the English printing.

XI

(1926)

MANTRAP / BY / SINCLAIR LEWIS / [*publishers' seal*] / New York / HARCOURT, BRACE AND COMPANY

Cr. 8vo ($7\frac{7}{16} \times 5$).

COLLATION: Half-title, list of eight Novels by Sinclair Lewis, title as above, copyright notice of five lines and printers' notice of three lines, dedication To Frazier Hunt, blank, text pp. 7–308, two blank leaves.

BINDING: Medium blue cloth, stamped in orange.

THE first dust wrapper contains no excerpts from reviews of this book. 84,952 copies were sold by the publisher up to November 5, 1930.

Mantrap was serialized in *Collier's Weekly*, February 13, 1926, to May 8, 1926, inclusive.

XII

(1926)

John Dos Passos' / MANHATTAN TRANSFER / By / Sinclair Lewis / Author of "Main Street," "Babbitt," / "Arrowsmith," Etc. / [*publishers' seal*] / New York and London / Harper & Brothers Publishers / Mcmxxvi

Small Fcap 4to.

COLLATION: 21 pp., frontispiece, plate opposite p. 2.

BINDING: Light green boards, cloth spine and corners; paper label on front cover.

COLOPHON states edition limited to nine hundred and seventy-five copies of which eight hundred and seventy-five are for distribution in America.

This review is reprinted in part from the *Saturday Review of Literature*.

Entirely out of print.

III

XIII

(1927)

ELMER GANTRY / BY / SINCLAIR LEWIS / [*publishers' decoration*] / NEW YORK / HAR-COURT, BRACE AND COMPANY

Cr. 8vo.

COLLATION: Half-title, list of nine Novels by Sinclair Lewis, title as above, copyright (dated 1927), dedication To H. L. Mencken with profound admiration, blank, note by S. L., blank, text pp. 1–432.

BINDING: Blue cloth, stamped in orange.

FIRST BINDING (20,000 copies) of the first edition (100,000 copies) has on the backbone a G that looks like a C in the title.

Up to November 5, 1930, 343,203 copies had been sold in America.

XIV

(1928)

THE MAN / WHO KNEW COOLIDGE /
Being the Soul of Lowell Schmaltz, / Constructive
and Nordic Citizen / BY / SINCLAIR LEWIS /
[*publishers' seal*] / NEW YORK / HARCOURT,
BRACE AND COMPANY

Cr. 8vo ($7\frac{1}{2} \times 5\frac{1}{16}$).

COLLATION: Half-title, list of ten Novels by
Sinclair Lewis, title as above, copyright notice of
two lines and printers' notice of three lines, dedication of five lines, blank, Contents, blank, division
title, blank, text pp. 11–275, blank, two blank
leaves.

BINDING: Medium blue cloth, stamped in orange.

THE first dust wrapper contains no excerpts from
reviews of this book. The first printing consisted
of 30,000 copies; 20,000 copies were sold at the reg-
ular price, and the balance was remaindered. The
book is again in print in the Nobel Prize Edition.

XV

(1929)

DODSWORTH / a Novel by / SINCLAIR LEWIS / [*publishers' seal*] / HARCOURT, BRACE AND COMPANY / NEW YORK

Cr. 8vo ($7\frac{1}{2} \times 5\frac{1}{8}$).

COLLATION: Half-title, list of eleven Novels by Sinclair Lewis, title as above, copyright of three lines (Published, March, 1929) and two-line printers' notice, dedication To Dorothy, blank, text pp. 7–377, verso blank.

BINDING: Blue cloth, stamped in orange. The blue is a shade darker than that of the *Mantrap* binding.

THE first dust wrapper does not contain excerpts from reviews of this book.

The first printing consisted of 50,000 copies.

On November 5, 1930, 91,895 copies had been sold by Harcourt, Brace.

An advance issue of 900 copies only ($7\frac{1}{2} \times 5\frac{1}{8}$) was issued for the book trade. It is in orange cloth with top stained black; spine lettering blind. Before the title is a tipped-in notice: This is a Special Edition Presented / to the Trade in Advance of Publi- / cation and is not for sale. /.

It is reasonably scarce in good condition.

XVI

(1929)

CHEAP and CONTENTED / LABOR / The
Picture of a Southern / Mill Town in 1929 / by /
Sinclair Lewis / Author of "Main Street", /
"Babbitt", / Dodsworth", Etc. / By permission
of / Sinclair Lewis and the Scripps-Howard
Newspapers / Copyright, 1929, by United Feature
Syndicate, Inc. / .

Cr. 8vo, thin ($8\frac{3}{8} \times 5\frac{1}{2}$), stapled.

COLLATION: Title, verso with reproduction from
photograph, Introduction (page numbered at top),
conclusion of Introduction, text pp. 5–32.
Photographic reproductions: inside front cover,
verso of title, p. [23].

BINDING: Stiff blue wrappers, decoration on
front cover by Becker.

THE first issue, collated above, does not have the
first quotation marks about Dodsworth on title;

116

it is numbered at top of page 3 with running head; page 5 numbered at top with running head and no text heading.

Of the 25,000 or more copies of this booklet issued there were at least several hundred of the first issue released. Many copies of this issue, it has been found, were distributed in the South among the workers. Several hundred have been recently uncovered in a New York storage house.

Mr. Lewis states that no further copies will be issued.

XVII

(1931)

NOBEL PRIZE ADDRESS

WHY SINCLAIR LEWIS / GOT THE NOBEL
PRIZE / ADDRESS BY / ERIK AXEL KARL-
FELDT / Permanent Secretary of the Swedish
Academy / AT THE / NOBEL FESTIVAL /
December 10, 1930 / AND / ADDRESS by
SINCLAIR LEWIS / BEFORE THE SWEDISH
ACADEMY / December 12, 1930 / [*ornament*] /
HARCOURT, BRACE AND COMPANY / 383
Madison Avenue, New York

Med. 8vo ($9\frac{1}{4} \times 6\frac{1}{8}$).

COLLATION: Title, blank, text of address by
Karlfeldt pp. 1–8, Address by Sinclair Lewis pp.
9–21, list of books By Sinclair Lewis which omits
The Man Who Knew Coolidge.

BINDING: Light brown stiff wrappers.

FOR quick reference the first edition can be determined by the lack of Sinclair Lewis's footnote p. 1, and the title *The Man Who Knew Coolidge* is lacking from the list of Lewis's books at the end of the volume.

The first printing consisted of 3,000 copies; 2,000 of which were burned at the request of Sinclair Lewis. The 1,000 copies were distributed to dealers.

XVIII

(1931)

Title: same as first edition.

Med. 8vo ($9\frac{1}{4} \times 6\frac{1}{8}$).

COLLATION: Title same as first edition, blank, text of address by Karlfeldt, pp. 1–8, with footnote by Sinclair Lewis p. 1, The American Fear of Literature, an address by Sinclair Lewis, pp. 9–23, list of books By Sinclair Lewis with *The Man Who Knew Coolidge* added, blank leaf.

BINDING: Light brown stiff wrappers.

THIS revised edition, published in May, 1931, contains many additions and corrections made by Lewis. There is a footnote by Lewis p. 1. Some of the interesting changes are:

Shaw's name has been removed and that of

Knut Hamsun added in the list near the bottom of p. 14. The author states that the reason for this was that there were too many Englishmen in the list.

Twenty words have been added following "University of Chicago" bottom of p. 17.

Ninety words have been added following the words "to comprehend them" bottom of p. 19.

These are but a few of the interesting changes made from the earlier text over which Lewis had no supervision. The first edition was printed from the cabled report which was published in the New York *Times*.

The first printing of this revised edition consisted of 2,000 copies.

XIX

(1931)

NOBEL PRIZE ADDRESS
FIRST SEPARATE PRINTING

LES PRIX NOBEL / EN 1930 / [*rule*] / THE AMERICAN FEAR / OF LITERATURE / NOBEL ADDRESS DELIVERED IN STOCK-HOLM, / DECEMBER 12, 1930 / by / SIN-CLAIR LEWIS / Stockholm 1931 / Kungl. Boktryckeriet. P. A. Norstedt & Soner / 310369 /. Front cover used as title.

Med. 8vo (9¾ × 6½).

COLLATION: Text pp. 1–12.

BINDING: Stiff white wrappers.

THIS edition, in English, was printed without the Address of Erik Axel Karlfeldt.

X X

(1931)

A LETTER TO CRITICS.

Three-column broadside ($16\frac{1}{2} \times 12\frac{1}{2}$) printed in black on yellow paper, decorations in orange about press imprint, and head and foot pieces.

375 copies only issued for the members of the American Booksellers Association by The Stephen Daye Press of Brattleboro, Vermont. Designed by Vrest Orton.

PROOFS of this printing were sent to Mr. Lewis October 21, 1931. First copy received by the bibliographer October 21. Mr. Lewis stated that there were to be some textual changes in the Stephen Daye printing; they were not made in the first printing.

On September 27, 1931, Mr. Lewis gave Stanford University Press permission to print an edition of twenty-five or thirty copies only. This has not been seen; it followed the edition described above.

XXI

(1932)

Sinclair Lewis / On / The Valley of the Moon / [*decoration*] / .

French folder, $(7\frac{1}{8} \times 5\frac{1}{8})$, front page used as title, verso contains colophon: Of this first edition one hundred copies / have been issued by the Harvard Press / for private distribution by Harvey Taylor /, blank, text of Lewis's review of Jack London's novel, conclusion of text, followed by three blank pages.

Issued stapled, uncut, on paper water-marked Chanticleer.

One hundred numbered copies were issued signed by Harvey Taylor.

LEWIS's review is interesting in that he collaborated with Jack London, at about this period, on a number of stories published in book form but which he did not bother to investigate as partly his own.

XXII

(1932)

LAUNCELOT / BY / SINCLAIR LEWIS / [*decoration*] / .

Eight-page pamphlet (8 × 5¾), stapled.

Inside front cover contains colophon stating that this first edition of the earliest known published literary writing by Sinclair Lewis consists of one hundred copies privately printed by the Harvard Press for Harvey Taylor. Page 3 blank, pp. 4 and 5 contain the text with a note at the end stating that it was previously printed in the *Yale Literary Magazine*, March, 1904. The text is signed H. S. Lewis, as it was originally.

The edition was limited to 100 copies only, signed and numbered by Harvey Taylor, and three review copies.

The item seems to be scarce, probably owing to my carelessness or to my too thorough maid. I cannot locate a copy for a complete description.

CONTRIBUTIONS TO BOOKS

(A)

(1912)

JOHN AMES MITCHELL The Man Who is Responsible for "Life" New York: Frederick A. Stokes, 1912.

Med. 8vo, 15 pp., wrappers.

John Ames Mitchell, Novelist, Editor and Artist, by Sinclair Lewis, pp. 3–6.

(Reprinted, from the same plates, from *The Book News Monthly*, March, 1912.)

Entirely out of print.

(B)

(1913)

HISTORY OF THE CLASS OF 1907 YALE
COLLEGE   Edited by Thomas A. Tully, Class
Secretary [New Haven, Conn., 1913]

In the biographies of the members of the Class
of 1907 there is a quotation from an autobiographical letter from Sinclair Lewis, pp. 180–81.

Issued in dark blue cloth.

Entirely out of print.

(C)

(1915)

IRVIN COBB HIS BOOK Friendly tributes
from a dinner tendered to Irvin Shrewsbury Cobb
at the Waldorf-Astoria Hotel, New York, April
twenty-fifth, 1915.

Royal 8vo, 27 unnumbered pp., plates and
mounted caricature, boards with paper label on
front cover.

C-O-B-B, by Sinclair Lewis, pp. [4]–[6].

Entirely out of print.

(D)

(1915)

HUGH WALPOLE A Series of Sketches of a
Great New Novelist New York: George H. Doran,
[1915]
  Back cover used as title.
  Thin Cr. 8vo, 32 pp., port. on inside front cover,
list of six Novels by Hugh Walpole on inside rear
cover.
  *Who Is Hugh Walpole and Why Should You
Read Him?* by Sinclair Lewis, pp. 1–4.
  Entirely out of print.

(E)

(1918)

THE BEST SHORT STORIES OF 1918   Edited
by Edward J. O'Brien   Boston: Small, Maynard
& Company [1918]
  Cr. 8vo, 441 pp., cloth.
  The Willow Walk, a story, by Sinclair Lewis,
pp. 154–170. (Reprinted from *Saturday Evening
Post*, August 10, 1918).

(F)

(1920)

JURGEN AND THE CENSOR   Report of the
Emergency Committee Organized to Protest
Against the Suppression of James Branch Cabell's
JURGEN

Privately Printed for the Emergency Committee,
New York, 1920.

Cr. 8vo, 77 pp., cloth.

A letter from Sinclair Lewis, p. 43.

485 copies only.

(G)

(1921)

My / Maiden Effort [*in red*] / Being the Personal
Confessions of / Well-known American Authors /
As to their Literary Beginnings / With an Intro-
duction / by / Gelett Burgess / [*publishers' seal
in red*] / Published for / The Authors' League of
America / by / Doubleday, Page & Company /
Garden City, N. Y., and Toronto / 1921 /.

Cr. 8vo ($7\frac{7}{16}$ × 5). The first edition so states on
copyright page.

Issued in dark blue cloth, stamped in gilt.

Sinclair Lewis's letter, pp. 138–139, relating to
his article "Did Mrs. Thurston Get the Idea of
'The Masquerader' from Mr. Zangwill?" which
appeared in *The Critic*, June, 1905.

(H)

(1924)

THESE UNITED STATES   A Symposium
Edited by Ernest Gruening   Second Series   New
York: Boni & Liveright, [1924]

Cr. 8vo. 439 pp.

Minnesota, the Norse State, by Sinclair Lewis,
pp. 20–33. (Reprinted from *The Nation,* May 30,
1923).

Out of print, 1931.

(I)

(1925)

Short Stories / Edited By / H. C. Schweikert /
Central High School / St. Louis, Missouri /
[*publishers' seal*] / New York / Harcourt, Brace
and Company /.

12mo, 521 pp. Issued in wine cloth, stamped in
yellow.

The copyright page, dated 1925, does not contain reprint notice.

Sinclair Lewis's short story, Young Man Axelbrod, appears on pp. 159–173, with biographical
note pp. 158–159, and questions for students,
pp. 173–174. (Young Man Axelbrod reprinted
from *Century Magazine*, June, 1917; XCIV: pp.
188–198. It is also found in *Golden Book*, March,
1931.)

(J)

(1925)

FOUR DAYS ON THE WEBUTUCK RIVER
By Charles E. Benton   With an Introduction by
Sinclair Lewis   Troutbeck Leaflet Number Six
Amenia (New York): Privately Printed at the
Troutbeck Press, July, 1925.

Demy 8vo, 20 pp., thin brown double wrappers.
200 copies only printed.

The Introduction, pp. [5]–[6], is by Sinclair
Lewis.

Entirely out of print.

(K)

(1929)

On Parade / Caricatures By / Eva Herrmann /
[*decoration*] / Edited by Erich Posselt / Contributions / By / Prominent Authors / 1929 / Coward-
McCann New York /.

   [*Above title in woodcut*]

   Cr. 4to (9⅝ × 7). No reprint notice on copyright
page. Issued in green boards, black cloth spine.
Lettering on front cover black and blue, spine gilt.

   Sinclair Lewis's one-page autobiographical note,
p. 96, with caricature p. 97, and a list of his books
p. 99.

(L)

(1930)

LITERARY TREASURES OF 1929   Published
by Hearst's International Cosmopolitan Magazine for private distribution only.

Med. 8vo, 309 numbered pp., buckram.

He Had a Brother, a story, by Sinclair Lewis,
pp. 74–103. (Reprinted from *The Cosmopolitan*,
June, 1929).

3,000 copies only printed.

(M)

(1930)

The [in red] / 1930 / American [in red] / Scrap Book / Forum Press [in red] / New York /.

Border design on top and fore edge red and black.

Copyright page states: First Printed, January, 1930.

Issued in blue cloth, stamped in red and gilt.

Contains Sinclair Lewis's "Stars and Stripes" pp. 88–89.

(Reprinted from *Pictorial Review*, June, 1929; XXX: p. 14, where it appeared under title "Is America a Paradise for Women?") The companion article by Dorothy Thompson (Mrs. Sinclair Lewis) is contained on pp. 90–92. (Also reprinted from *Pictorial Review* of the same date as above noted.)

(N)

(1931)

THE O-SA-GE, 1931. Published by the Senior High School, Sauk Centre, Minnesota, 1931.

Imp. 8vo, 132 pp., incl. plates and division sheets.

The Long Arm of the Small Town, by Sinclair Lewis, p. 83, port.

Lewis is in the group picture of the Class of 1902, p. 79.

350 copies only printed.

(O)

(1931)

VERMONT PROSE A Miscellany Edited by
Arthur Wallace Peach and Harold Goddard Rugg.
The Green Mountain Series. Brattleboro [Ver-
mont]: Stephen Daye Press [1931]

Cr. 8vo, 256 pp., buckram.

Contains a report of an address delivered before
the Rutland Rotary Club, September 23, 1929.

(Reprinted from the Rutland *Daily Herald*,
September 24, 1929.)

A letter from Lewis regarding the account of his
talk acts as an introduction.

(P)

(1931)

Front cover used as title: Opinions / On The Amenities of Book-Collecting / As Expressed by a Group / of Seasoned Bibliophiles / On the Occasion of the / Printing of / Catalogue One Hundred / [*decoration*] / Dauber & Pine Bookshops, Inc. / 66 Fifth Avenue New York City / Near Twelfth Street Algonquin 4–7880 / Open Till Ten P. M. /.

(7 × 6)

Issued December 1, 1931. 13 pp. text, rear cover and verso of front cover blank.

Contains a short letter by Sinclair Lewis, p. (7), of no interest. Also contains letters from William Rose Benét, Joseph Hergesheimer, Christopher Morley, Vincent Starrett, and others.

CONTRIBUTIONS TO
PERIODICALS

CONTRIBUTIONS TO
PERIODICALS

(1) Yale *Courant*, May 21, 1904. Vol. XL: 389.
A SONG OF PRINCE HAL, a poem.

(2) Yale *Courant*, June 4, 1904. XL: 425.
STUDENT LIED, a poem in German.

(3) Yale *Courant*, June 4, 1904. XL: 436.
PUCK TO QUEEN MAB, a poem.

(4) Yale *Courant*, June 18, 1904. XL: 462.
A MAY TIME CAROL, a poem.

(5) Yale *Courant*, June 18, 1904. XL: 463.
THE COWARD MINSTREL, a story.

(6) Yale *Literary Magazine*, October, 1904. LXX: 26.
ODYSSEUS AT OGYGIA, a poem.

(7) Yale *Courant*, October 15, 1904. XLI: 20.
HALLOWE'EN, a poem.

(8) Yale *Courant*, October 15, 1904. XLI: 1.
FATHER AMBROSIAL, a story.

(9) Yale *Courant*, October 29, 1904. XLI: 52.
UM EIN UND ZWANZIG, a poem in German.

(10) Yale *Literary Magazine*, December, 1904.
LXX: 98–99.
THE THIRD ESTATE, a poem.

(11) Yale *Courant*, December 10, 1904. XLI: 82.
THE SEVENTH TROOP, a poem.

(12) Yale *Courant*, December 10, 1904. XLI: 88.
THE ROYAL GLAMOUR, a story.

(13) Yale *Courant*, December 24, 1904. XLI: 125.
THE FIREFLIES, a poem.

(14) Yale *Courant*, December 24, 1904. XLI: 117.
WHEN VIZIERS SPEAK, a poem.

(15) Yale *Literary Magazine*, February, 1905.
LXX: 184–187.
BEHIND THE ARRAS, a Christmas masque.

(16) Yale *Courant*, February 11, 1905. XLI: 188.
A NE'ER-DO-WEEL, a poem.

(17) Yale *Courant*, February 11, 1905. XLI: 189.
CONCERNING PSYCHOLOGY, a story.

(18) Yale *Courant*, March 25, 1905. XLI: 264.
A MIRACLE, FORSOOTH, a story.

(19) Yale *Literary Magazine*, April, 1905. LXX:
271.
THE YELLOW STREAK, a story.

(20) Yale *Courant*, April 8, 1905. XLI: 286.
A SUMMER'S TALE, a poem.

(21) *The Critic*, June, 1905. XLVI: 551.
DID MRS. THURSTON GET THE IDEA OF
"THE MASQUERADER" FROM MR. ZANG-
WILL? an article.

(22) Yale *Courant*, October 12, 1905. XLII: 64.
AN ELEMENTARY COURSE IN EROTICS, a
story.

(23) Yale *Literary Magazine*, November, 1905.
LXXI: 44–52.
THE LONELINESS OF THEODORE, a story.

(24) Yale *Courant*, November 24, 1905. XLII: 99.
FATHER KILEEN, a poem.

(25) *Pacific Monthly*, November, 1905.
MATSU-NO-KATA, a story.

(26) Yale *Literary Magazine*, January, 1906.
LXXI: 154.
THE HEART OF POPE INNOCENT, a story.

(27) Yale *Courant*, March 3, 1906. XLII: 284.
SAINT HUBERT, a poem.

(28) Yale *Monthly Magazine*, April, 1906. I: 220–
228.
A THEORY OF VALUES, a story.

(29) Yale *Literary Magazine*, April, 1906. LXXI: 287.
EDITOR'S TABLE, an editorial.

(30) *The Housekeeper* (Minneapolis), April, 1906.
AT LIGHTING TIME, a poem.

(31) Yale *Literary Magazine*, May, 1906. LXXI: 333.
EDITOR'S TABLE, an editorial.

(32) Yale *Literary Magazine*, June, 1906. LXXI: 335.
UNKNOWN UNDERGRADUATES, an editorial.

(33) Yale *Literary Magazine*, June, 1906. LXXI: 374.
EDITOR'S TABLE, an editorial.

(34) *The Housekeeper*, June, 1906. No vol. or p. available.
A CROONING LULLABY, a poem.

(35) Yale *Literary Magazine*, November, 1906. LXII: 80.
EDITOR'S TABLE, an editorial.

(36) Yale *Courant*, November, 1906. XLIII: 47.
EXIT HOMO, a poem.

(37) Yale *Literary Magazine*, December, 1906. LXXII: 83.
IN PRAISE OF SOUTH MIDDLE, an editorial.

BIBLIOGRAPHY

(38) Yale *Literary Magazine*, December, 1906. LXXII: 126.
EDITOR'S TABLE, an editorial.

(39) *Woman's Home Companion*, December, 1906.
JANUARY NIGHTS, a poem.

(40) *Reader Magazine*, December, 1906. IX: 65.
DECEMBER MAYING, a poem.

(41) Yale *Literary Magazine*, January, 1907. LXXII: 166.
EDITOR'S TABLE, an editorial.

(42) *The Outer's Book*, February, 1907.
FAERIES O' THE LAKE, a poem.

(43) *Mayflower*, 1907.
SLEEPY HEAD TOP, a poem.

(44) *The Outer's Book*, 1907.
NE'ER DO WELL.

(45) Yale *Literary Magazine*, February, 1907. LXXII: 212.
EDITOR'S TABLE, an editorial.

(46) *Woman's Home Companion*, 1907.
THE ALARM CLOCK, a poem.

(47) *The Outer's Book*, March, 1907.
CURLY TAILED PUP AND ME, a poem.

(48) *The Housekeeper*, March, 1907.
THE GAS STOVE BEAST, a poem.

(49) Yale *Literary Magazine*, March, 1907. LXXII: 268.
A RONDEAU OF FAREWELL, a poem.

(50) *Puck*, March 27, 1907.
CANNED POETRY, a poem.

(52) *The New Age*, April, 1907.
COURAGE, a poem.

(53) *Puck*, April 3, 1907.
THE COMPLETE DIALECT-WRITER, a poem.

(54) *The Outer's Book*, May, 1907.
MAY AFIELD, a poem.

(55) *Life*, May 2, 1907. P. 615.
A RAKING OF THE RAKERS, a paragraph article in "Literary Zoo."

(56) *The Blue Mule*, May, 1907.
A PASSAGE IN ISAIAH, a story.

(56a) *Puck*, May 9, 1907.
A RONDEAU OF SORROW, a poem.

(57) *Life*, May 23, 1907. P. 709.
THE CELTIC REVIVAL, a paragraph article.

(58) *Transatlantic Tales*, June, 1907. XXXV: 150.
DOWN HERE, a poem by Sully Prud-homme. Translated by Sinclair Lewis.

(59) *The Gray Goose*, June, 1907.
ART AND THE WOMAN, a story.

(60) *Smart Set*, July, 1907.
THE ULTRA-MODERN, a poem.

(61) *Life*, July 4, 1907. P. 13.
MÆCENAS WELCHES, a paragraph article in
"Literary Zoo."

(62) *The Housekeeper*, July, 1907.
THE GOOD SHIP "TEETER BOARD," a
poem.

(63) *Puck*, July 24, 1907.
EXTRACTS FROM A CLUB-WOMAN'S DIARY,
a humorous article.

(64) *The Outer's Book*, July, 1907.
NIMROD, JUNIOR, a poem.

(65) *New England Magazine*, July, 1907. XXXVI:
615.
THE QUATRAIN, a poem.

(66) *New England Magazine*, July, 1907. XXXVI:
557.
THE PASSING PANTOMIME, a poem. (Reprinted in *Literary Digest*.)

(67) *Transatlantic Tales*, July, 1907. XXXV: 90.
ECSTASY, a poem by Victor Hugo. Translated by Sinclair Lewis.

(68) *Life*, August 1, 1907. P. 131–33.
AMERICAN KIPLINGS, a paragraph article in
"Literary Zoo."

(69) *Smart Set*, August, 1907.
DIM HOURS OF DUSK, a poem.

(70) *Transatlantic Tales*, September, 1907. XXXV:
537.
THE SONG OF THE KING'S JESTER, by
Stuart Merrill, a poem translated by
Sinclair Lewis.

(71) *The Outer's Book*, September, 1907.
BALLADE FROM THE CITY, a poem.

(72) *The Outer's Book*, September, 1907.
THE OUTER'S SONG, a poem.

(73) New Orleans *Times-Democrat*, 1907.
CITY LONELINESS, a poem.

(74) *Transatlantic Tales*, September, 1907. XXXV:
578.
FLOCKI, REMARKABLE DOG, by Rudolf
Presber, a story translated by Sinclair
Lewis.

(75) *The Book News Monthly*, September, 1907.
TO WILLIAM BUTLER YEATS, a poem.

(76) *Transatlantic Tales*, October, 1907. XXXVI:
748.
THE SEA OF CITIES, a poem by Detlev von
Liliencron. Translated by Sinclair Lewis.

(77) *Transatlantic Tales*, October, 1907. XXXVI: 726.

LITTLE DRUMMER OF THE BLUES, a story by Charles Foley. Translated by Sinclair Lewis.

(78) *Transatlantic Tales*, October, 1907. XXXVI: 734.

CHERRIES OF PROVENCE, a story by Leo Larguier. Translated by Sinclair Lewis.

(79) *Transatlantic Tales*, October, 1907. XXXVI: 749.

A GAMBLER OF A NIGHT, a story by Paul Bourget. Translated by Sinclair Lewis.

(80) *Home Magazine*, October, 1907.

HALLOWE'EN, a poem.

(81) *Puck*, October 23, 1907.

THE AFFININGS OF AN AFFINITIST, a humorous article.

(82) *Life*, October 10, 1907. P. 414.

EDITORS WHO WRITE, an article.

(83) *Transatlantic Tales*, November, 1907. XXXVII: 51.

THE SHORE, a poem by Theodore Storm. Translated by Sinclair Lewis.

(84) *The Circle*, November, 1907.

HIPPOPOTAMUS, a poem.

(85) *Transatlantic Tales*, November, 1907.
XXXVII: 83.
CRADLE SONG, a poem by Detlev von
Liliencron. Translated by Sinclair Lewis.

(86) *Pacific Monthly*, November, 1907. XVIII:
609.
THE STRUGGLE, a poem.

(87) *Transatlantic Tales*, December, 1907.
XXXVII: 195.
MOON OF NIGHT, a poem by Martin Gries.
Translated by Sinclair Lewis.

(88) *Transatlantic Tales*, December, 1907.
XXXVII: 207.
THE SNARE, a story by Paul Bourget.
Translated by Sinclair Lewis.

(89) *Smart Set*, December, 1907. XXIII: 130.
DISILLUSION, a poem.

(90) *Youth's Companion* (Boston), December 19,
1907.
BEFORE CHRISTMAS, a poem.

(91) *New Idea*, 1908.
ON WASH BOWL SEA, a poem.

(92) *Transatlantic Tales*, January, 1908. XXXVII:
328.
DERELICT, a story by Jean Reibrach.
Translated by Sinclair Lewis.

(93) *Overland Monthly*, January, 1908. LI: 51.
My California Lady, a poem. (Reprinted in *Overland Monthly*, July, 1926.)

(94) *Overland Monthly*, January, 1908. LI: 82.
Gold in Umber, a poem. (Reprinted in *Overland Monthly*, June, 1926.)

(95) *The Housekeeper*, February, 1908.
Big Brother the Wise, a poem.

(96) *The New Age*, March, 1908.
The Fountain Spirit, a poem.

(97) *The New Age*, March, 1908.
The City Fountain, a poem.

(98) *The Housekeeper*, May, 1908.
The May Baskets, a poem.

(99) *Woman's Home Companion*, May, 1908.
The Awful Jungle, a poem.

(100) *Holland's Magazine*, May, 1908.
Making Faces, a poem.

(101) *Puck*, May 13, 1908.
Wailing and Fixing of Teeth, a two-page humorous monologue.

(102) *Puck*, June 24, 1908.
The Butt, story-article.

(103) *The New Age*, August, 1908.
The Mystery, a poem.

(104) *Century Magazine*, September, 1908. LXXVI: 798.
MY LADY'S MAID, a poem.

(105) *The Outer's Book*, September, 1908.
THE CLERGYMAN WHO FISHES, an editorial.

(106) *The Outer's Book*, October, 1908.
TETHER BALL, an editorial.

(107) *The Open Court*, September, 1908.
THE SPIRIT'S CALL, a poem.

(108) *The Delineator*, November, 1908.
THE DEATH-A-COLD, a poem.

(109) *The Designer*, January, 1909.
WHERE FIREFLIES GROW, a poem.

(110) *The Peoples' Magazine*, February, 1909.
SUMMER IN WINTER, a poem.

(111) *The Red Book*, May, 1909.
THEY THAT TAKE THE SWORD, a story.

(112) *The Designer*, June, 1909.
MY POLICEMAN, a poem.

(112a) *The Nautilus*, August, 1909.
THE SMILE LADY, a story.

(112b) San Francisco *Bulletin*, September 21, 1909.
A. "Irish Chink" frightens off burglars and saves block.

B. Transport's mate tries to shoot his wife.

C. Review of light opera at the Princess Theatre.

(112c) *The Nautilus*, October, 1909, to May, 1910.
THE CITY SHADOW, a serial story.

(113) San Francisco *Bulletin*, October 23, 1909.
THE MASQUE OF GASPAR'S PASSING, a poem.

(114) *Sunset* Magazine, January, 1910. XXIV: 3–8.
POLLY, a story.

(115) *Sunset* Magazine, April, 1910.
ONE TAKES HIS EASE, a story.

(116) *Sunset* Magazine, April, 1910. XXIV: 432–39.
SAN FRANCISCO'S PLEASURE CURE, an article.

(117) *Volta Review*, July, 1910. XII: 228.
THE OUTLOOK FOR THE BLIND, a book review.

(118) *Volta Review*, October, 1910. XII: 453.
BOOKS FOR THE CLASS ROOM, a book review.

(119) *Volta Review*, October, 1910. XII: 454.
PROTOPLASM AND THE SOUL, a book review.

(120) *Volta Review*, October, 1910. XII: 454.
TWO WRITING MANUALS, a book review.

(121) *Volta Review*, October, 1910. XIII: 544.
ZENATA, a book review.

(122) *The Bellman* (Minneapolis), May, 1911.
THE WAY TO ROME, a story.

(123) *Puck*, May 17, 1911.
A COURSE IN HEROISM, humorous article.

(124) *Ainslee's Magazine*, 1912.
A CANTICLE OF GREAT LOVERS, a poem.

(125) *Short Stories*, August, 1912. P. 37–42.
LOKI, THE RED, a story.

(126) *Short Stories*, March, 1913. P. 92.
SCENTED SPRING AND THE G. P., a story.

(126a) Baltimore *News*, August 20, 1913.
HOOP-SKIRT DAYS, an article.

(126b) St. Louis *Republic*, October 25, 1913.
P. 1, Col. 6. America is sex mad.
P. 1, Col. 7. Review of D. H. Lawrence's
Sons and Lovers.
P. 1, Col. 6. Important translation.
P. 2, Col. 1. Kate D. Wiggins loves the
farm.
P. 6, Col. 3. Kangaroo Kid hero of South
Seas.

(126c) *Ladies' World*, July, 1914.
THE SINGING MEN, a poem.

(127) *The Bookman*, November, 1914. XL: 280–286.
THE PASSING OF CAPITALISM, an article.

(128) *Saturday Evening Post*, October 2, 1915. CLXXXVIII: 10.
NATURE, INC., a story.

(129) *Saturday Evening Post*, October 30, 1915. CLXXXVIII: 6.
COMMUTATION: $9.17, a story.

(130) *Saturday Evening Post*. November 27, 1915. CLXXXVIII: 11.
THE OTHER SIDE OF THE HOUSE, a story.

(130a) Baker & Taylor's *Christmas Bulletin*, 1915.
THE HOME WITHOUT BOOKS, an article.

(131) *The Red Book*, June, 1917.
THE GHOST PATROL, a story. Reprinted in the *Famous Story Magazine*, May, 1926. P. 263.

(132) *Saturday Evening Post*, January 1, 1916. CLXXXVII: 5; 14.
IF I WERE BOSS, a story.

(133) *Smart Set*, August, 1916. P. 41.
I'M A STRANGER HERE MYSELF, a story.

(134) *Everybody's Magazine*, October, 1916. XXXV: 468.
HE LOVED HIS COUNTRY, a story.

(135) *Saturday Evening Post*, October 14, 1916. CLXXXIX: 28.
HONESTLY IF POSSIBLE, a story.

(136) *Saturday Evening Post*, February 17, 1917. CLXXXIX: 15.
TWENTY-FOUR HOURS IN JUNE, a story.

(137) *Metropolitan Magazine*, March 17, 1917. XLV: 15.
THE POINSETTIA WIDOW, a story.

(138) *Saturday Evening Post*, March 17, 1917. CLXXXIX: 8.
A STORY WITH A HAPPY ENDING, a story.

(139) *Saturday Evening Post*, April 7, 1917. CLXXXIX: 3.
HOBOHEMIA, a story. (See sequel October 20.)

(140) *Metropolitan Magazine*, June, 1917. XLVI: 21.
THE SCARLET SIGN, a story.

(142) *Saturday Evening Post*, July 28, 1917. CXC: 11.
A WOMAN BY CANDLE-LIGHT, a story.

(143) *Metropolitan Magazine*, August, 1917. XLVI: 7.
SNAPPY DISPLAY, a story.

(144) *Saturday Evening Post*, August 11, 1917. CXC: 14.
THE WHISPERER, a story.

(145) *Good Housekeeping*, September, 1917. LXV: 25–28.
THE HIDDEN PEOPLE, a story.

(146) *Metropolitan Magazine*, October, 1917. XLVI: 12.
BLACK SNOW AND ORANGE SKY, a story.

(147) *McClure's Magazine*, October, 1917. XLIX: 27.
FOR THE ZELDA BUNCH, a story.

(148) *Saturday Evening Post*, October 20, 1917. CXC: 63.
JOY-JOY, a story. (Sequel to "Hobohemia.")

(149) *Collier's Weekly*, January 19, 1918. LX: 14.
AFTERGLOW, a story.

(150) *Hearst's Magazine*, February, 1918. XLVII: 108.
TAMARACK LOVER, a story. (Reprinted November, 1931, Tower Magazines (Woolworth.)

(151) *Metropolitan Magazine,* February, 1918. XLVII: 19.
SPIRITUALIST VAUDEVILLE, an article.

(152) *McClure's Magazine,* February, 1918. LI: 17–18.
A ROSE FOR LITTLE EVA, a story.

(153) *Metropolitan Magazine,* March, 1918. XLVII: 26.
SLIP IT TO 'EM, a story.

(154) *Every Week,* March 30, 1918. VI: 7–10.
DETOUR—ROADS ROUGH, a story.

(155) *Every Week,* June 1, 1918. P. 6.
AN INVITATION TO TEA, a story.

(156) *Saturday Evening Post,* June 22, 1918. CXC: 5.
THE SHADOWY GLASS, a story.

(157) *Ladies' Home Journal,* July, 1918. XXXV: 13.
A WIDOWER FOR A WHILE, a story.

(158) *Metropolitan Magazine,* September, 1918. XLVIII: 12.
GETTING HIS BIT, a story.

(159) *Saturday Evening Post,* September 21, 1918. CXCI: 5.
THE SWEPT HEARTH, a story.

(160) *Metropolitan Magazine*, October, 1918. XLVII: 23.
Jazz, a story.

(161) *Popular Magazine*, October 7, 1918. L: 145.
Gladvertising, a story.

(162) *Saturday Evening Post*, January 11, 1919. CXCI: 5.
Moths in the Arc Light, a story.

(163) *Saturday Evening Post*, February 15, 1919. CXCI: 9.
The Shrinking Violet, a story.

(164) *Saturday Evening Post*, February 22, 1919. CXCI: 8.
Things, a story.

(165) *Saturday Evening Post*, April 19, 1919. CXCI: 5.
The Cat of the Stars, a story.

(166) *Saturday Evening Post*, May 24, 1919. CXCI: 5.
The Watcher Across the Road, a story.

(167) *Metropolitan Magazine*, June, 1919. L: 30.
Might and Millions, a story.

(168) *Pictorial Review*, June, 1919. P. 10.
The Kidnapped Memorial, a story.

(169) *Saturday Evening Post*, August 9, 1919.
CXCII: 8.
THE ENCHANTED HOUR, a story.

(170) *The Red Book*, June, 1919.
SPEED. a story. (Reprinted in *Famous Stories Magazine*, November, 1925. P. 263.)

(171) *The Red Book*, August, 1919.
THE SHRIMP-COLOURED BLOUSE, a story.

(172) *Saturday Evening Post*, December 13, 1919.
CXCII: 12.
BRONZE BARS, a story.

(173) *Saturday Evening Post*, December 20, 27, 1919; January 3, 1920. CXCII: 5, 24, 20.
ADVENTURES IN AUTOMOBUMMING, an article.

(174) *Saturday Evening Post*, January 24, 1920.
CXCII: 10–11.
HABEAS CORPUS, a story.

(175) *Saturday Evening Post*, May 29, 1920.
CXCII: 14–15.
THE WAY I SEE IT, a story.

(176) *Saturday Evening Post*, December 11, 1920.
CXCIII: 9–11.
THE GOOD SPORT, a story.

(177) *Harper's Magazine*, March, 1921. CXLII: 419–31.

A MATTER OF BUSINESS, a story. (Reprinted in *Golden Book*, July, 1929.)

(178) *American Magazine*, April, 1921. XCI: 17–19.

HOW I WROTE A NOVEL ON TRAINS AND BESIDE THE KITCHEN SINK, an article.

(179) *The Bookman*, May, 1921. LIII: 245.

FLOYD DELL, an article.

(180) *American Magazine*, May, 1921. XCI: 20.

NUMBER SEVEN TO SAGAPOOSE, a story.

(181) *Century Magazine*, May, 1921. CII: 1–18.

THE POST-MORTEM MURDER, a story.

(182) *The Red Book*, May, 1921. P. 47.

A CITIZEN OF THE MIRAGE, a story.

(183) *International Book Review*, December, 1922. I: 9.

A REVIEW OF REVIEWERS, an article.

(184) *Now and Then*, June, 1923. Pp. 17–18.

AUTHORS AND INTERVIEWING, an article.

(185) *The Nation*, August 29, 1923. CXVII: 211–13.

THE HACK DRIVER, a story.

(186) *The Nation*, June 4, 1924. CXVII: 631–32.
I Return to America, an article.

(187) *The Nation*, September 10, 1924. CXIX: 255.
Main Street's Been Paved, an article.

(188) *The Nation*, October 15, 22, 29, 1924. CXIX: 409, 437, 463.
Be Brisk with Babbitt, articles.

(189) *The Nation*, July 1, 1925. CXXI: 19.
An American Views the Huns, an article.

(190) *American Mercury*, October, 1925. VI: 129.
Self-Conscious America, an article.

(191) *The Nation*, December 9, 1925. CXXI: 662.
Can an Artist Live in America? an article.

(192) *New Statesman*, May 29, 1928. XXVII: 171.
Letter to the Pulitzer Prize Committee.

(192a) New York *Herald Tribune*, July 21 to September 29, 1928.
Sinclair Lewis Tours England, a series of twelve weekly letters published in the Sunday edition. The *Herald Tribune* combined the first two letters, thus cutting

their contents considerably. For a complete text see Minneapolis *Journal*.

(193) *The Nation*, July 25, 1928. CXXVII: 278.
Mr. Lorimer and Me, an article.

(194) *The Nation*, March 6, 1929. CXXVIII: 278.
Publicity Gone Mad, an article.

(195) *Advertising and Selling*, May 15, 1929. XIII: 17.
Sinclair Lewis Looks at Advertising, an article.

(196) *The Cosmopolitan*, June, 1929. LXXXVI: 17–18.
There Was a Prince, a story.

(198) *The Cosmopolitan*, July, 1929. LXXXVII: 68.
Elizabeth, Kitty and Jane, a story.

(199) *The Cosmopolitan*, August, 1929. LXXXVII: 64.
Dear Editor, a story.

(200) *The Cosmopolitan*, September, 1929. LXXXVII: 68.
What a Man! a story.

(201) *The Cosmopolitan*, October, 1929. LXXXVII: 40.
Keep Out of the Kitchen, a story.

(202) *The Cosmopolitan*, December, 1929. LXXXVII: 64.
A LETTER FROM THE QUEEN, a story.

(203) *The Nation*, December 18, 1929. CXXIV: 751.
DEVIL DOG RULE, an article.

(203a) *The Cosmopolitan*, February, 1930. LXXXVIII: 26–29, 122.
YOUTH, a story.

(204) *The Cosmopolitan*, August, 1930. LXXXIX: 40–3, 151.
A NOBLE EXPERIMENT, a story.

(205) *The Cosmopolitan*, September, 1930. LXXXIX: 42–4, 135.
BONGO, a story.

(206) *The Cosmopolitan*, December, 1930. LXXXIX: 52.
YOUNG MAN, GO EAST, a story.

(207) *The Cosmopolitan*, January, February, March, 1931. XC.
LET'S PLAY KING, a three-part serial story.

(208) *Saturday Evening Post*, June 6, 1931. CCIII: 3–5.
RING AROUND A ROSY, a story.

(209) *The Cosmopolitan*, July, 1931. XCII: 80.
      CITY OF MERCY, a story.

(210) *Saturday Evening Post*, September 12, 1931.
      CCIV: 3–5.
      LAND, a story.

(211) *Saturday Evening Post*, October 17, 24, 1931.
      CCIV: 3–5. CCIV: 16–17.
      DOLLAR CHASERS, a two-part story.

SELECTED BIOGRAPHICAL AND CRITICAL NOTICES IN BOOKS

SELECTED BIOGRAPHICAL AND CRITICAL NOTICES IN BOOKS

BECHOFER, [-ROBERTS], C. E. The Literary Renaissance in America. London [1923]. Pp. 105–14.
The book is dedicated to Sinclair Lewis.

BIRKHEAD, L. M. Is *Elmer Gantry* True? Girard, Kansas [1928]. 63 pp. Little Blue Book No. 1265. Contains a bibliography of material used in writing *Elmer Gantry*, pp. 14–16.

BOYNTON, PERCY HOLMES. More Contemporary Americans. Chicago: University of Chicago Press [1927].

BOYD, ERNEST A. Portraits. New York: Doran [1924].

CABELL, JAMES BRANCH. Sinclair Lewis: A Critical Essay. With a Foreword by Harvey Taylor.
Privately printed: New York, 1932.

FARRAR, JOHN (Editor). The Literary Spotlight. New York, 1924.

FOERSTER, NORMAN (Editor). The Reinterpretation of American Literature. New York, 1928.

FORSTER, E. M. Sinclair Lewis Interprets America. (Review of *Main Street*.)
Privately printed. New York: Harvard Press.
100 copies only numbered and signed by Harvey Taylor.

GORDON, GEORGE. The Men Who Make Our Novels. New York, 1919.
Pp. 223–27. Port.

HARRISON, OLIVER (pseud. for Harrison Smith). Sinclair Lewis. New York [1925?].
28 pp., plates, and mounted port. Decorated wrappers.
A later issue of 500 copies for Booksellers Association.

LEISY, E. E. American Literature: An Interpretive Survey. New York, 1929.

LEWIS, GRACE LIVINGSTON HEGGER. Half a Loaf (a novel). New York: Liveright, 1931.
The character Timothy Hale is supposed to be Sinclair Lewis. The author is the former wife of Mr. Lewis.

LIPPMANN, WALTER. Men of Destiny. New York: Macmillan, 1927.
Pp. 71–92.

MAIS, STUART PETER BRODIE. Some Modern Authors. London: Grant Richards, 1923.

MICHAUD, REGIS. The American Novel of Today. Boston: Little, Brown, 1928.
    "Sinclair Lewis and the Average Man," pp. 128–53.

MORGAN, LOUISE. Writers at Work. London: Chatto & Windus, 1931.
    Interview with Lewis, pp. 17–27.

PARRINGTON, VERNON LOUIS. Sinclair Lewis Our Own Diogenes. University of Washington Chapbook No. 5. Seattle, Washington, 1927.
    27 pp., wrappers over light boards.
    (Reprinted in *The Beginnings of Critical Realism in America*, 1860–1920. By V. L. Parrington. New York, 1930, Vol. 3.)

PATTEE, F. L. The New American Literature, 1890–1930. New York, 1930.

SEARCH-LIGHT (Frank, Waldo). Time Exposures. New York, 1926.

SHERMAN, STUART PRATT. The Significance of Sinclair Lewis. New York, 1922.
    20 pp. First issue on stiff brown wrappers with copyright notice on verso of cover.
    (Reprinted in *Now and Then*, June, 1923.)
    (Contained in *Points of View*, by Stuart P. Sherman, New York: Scribner's, 1924.)

STOKES, SEWELL. Pilloried! New York: Appleton, 1929.
"Main Street to Hollywood."

SQUIRE, JOHN COLLINGS. Contemporary American Authors. New York: Holt [1928].
Sinclair Lewis, by Milton Waldman, pp. 71–94.
(Reprinted from London *Mercury*, January, 1926.)

TANTE, DILLY. Living Authors. New York: Wilson, 1931.
Pp. 26–27. Port.

WEST, REBECCA. The Strange Necessity. Garden City: Doubleday, Doran, 1928.
"Sinclair Lewis Introduces Elmer Gantry."

WHIPPLE, THOMAS KING. Spokesmen: Modern Writers and American Life. New York: Appleton, 1928.
Pp. 208–29.

VAN DOREN, CARL. Contemporary American Novelists: 1900–1920. New York, 1922.
Pp. 161–64.

SELECTED BIOGRAPHICAL
AND CRITICAL NOTICES
IN PERIODICALS

SELECTED BIOGRAPHICAL AND CRITICAL NOTICES IN PERIODICALS

North American Review, June–September, 1922.

The Founding of Main Street (on the letters of Mrs. Trollope, Dickens, Thackeray, Matthew Arnold), by Stanley Thomas Williams.

Literary Review, September 16, 1922. P. 234.

Review of *Babbitt* by Carl Van Doren.

The Nation, September 20, 1922. Pp. 284–85.

Review of *Babbitt* by Ludwig Lewisohn.

The New Republic, October 11, 1922.

Sinclair Lewis, by Sherwood Anderson, pp. 172–73.

North American Review, November, 1922. 216:7.

Review of *Babbitt.*

Double Dealer, November, 1922. Pp. 245–47.

Review of *Babbitt* by William Thomas.

London *Bookman,* January, 1924. 65: 195–96.

How Sinclair Lewis Works, by M. Belgion.

The Bookman, April, 1925. Pp. 179–85.

The Salvation of Sinclair Lewis, by Grant Overton.

Arts and Decoration, May, 1925. 23: pp. 45, 86–87.
Sinclair Lewis, by Burton Rascoe.

Living Age, May 23, 1925. 325: 429–30.
John Bull and Sinclair Lewis.

Century Magazine, July, 1925. 110: 362–69.
Sinclair Lewis and Sherwood Anderson, by Carl Van Doren.

Living Age, May 15, 1926. 329: 381–82.
Arrowsmith in Germany.

The Nation, May 19, 1926. 122: 546.
Literary Main Street.

Outlook Magazine, July 6, 1927. 146: 307–308.
Honoré de Balzac and Sinclair Lewis, by L. F. Abbott.

Outlook Magazine, August 22, 1928.
Criticism of Patrick Kearney's dramatization of *Elmer Gantry* by F. R. Bellamy.

University of California Chronicle (Berkeley, California), 1928. 30: 417–27.
The Young Mr. Lewis, by Frances Theresa Russell. (See 1930 entry for continuation of article.)

The Bookman, March, 1929. 62: 52–53.
History of Sinclair Lewis' Books, by A. B. Maurice.

The Bookman, April, 1929. Pp. 191–92.
Review of *Dodsworth* by Ford Madox Ford.

The Nation, April 3, 1929. 128: 400 (1,000 words).
Review of *Dodsworth* by Carl Van Doren.

Sociology and Social Research, University of South-

ern California, Los Angeles, California, 1929. Vol.
14; pp. 174–80. Social distance in fiction: An an-
alysis of *Main Street*. By E. S. Bogardus.
University of California Chronicle, Berkeley, Cali-
fornia, 1930. Vol. 32: pp. 319–24.
The Growing Up of Sinclair Lewis, by Frances
Theresa Russell.
Catholic World, May, 1930. 132: 214–22.
The Future Significance of Sinclair Lewis.
Commonweal, November 19, 1930. 13: 61.
Babbitt Abroad.
Literary Digest, December 6, 1930. 107: 19.
British Views on Lewis's Prize.
Commonweal, December 10, 1930. 13: 147–49.
Success of *Main Street*. By E. Brace.
Current History, January, 1931. 33: 529–33.
America of Sinclair Lewis, by Lewis Mumford.
The Bookman, January, 1931. 72: 453–57.
Europe Looks at Sinclair Lewis.
New Review (Paris), January–February, 1931.
1: 46–52.
Sinclair Lewis, an American Phenomenon, by
V. F. Calverton.
Scribner's Magazine, March, 1931. 89: 325–28.
As I Like It, by William Lyon Phelps.
The Bookman, July, 1931. Pp. 487–88.
Sinclair Lewis, by Benjamin De Casseres.
Pictorial Review, April, 1931. 32: 17.
At the Court of King Gustaf (report of Nobel

Prize award), by Dorothy Thompson (Mrs. Sinclair Lewis.)
Liberty, October 10, 1931. 8: 15–18.

The Ghost of Jack London, by George Sylvester Viereck (from material discovered by Harvey Taylor, literary manager of the estate of Jack London).

Mr. Viereck's facts are wrong in that London used nine of Lewis's outline plots.
Saturday Evening Post, December 26, 1931. 204: 20–21.

Sinclair Lewis vs. His Education, by C. Gauss. Contains important facsimiles.

HARPER & BROTHERS'
CODE

It may be that earlier issues of the books published by Harper & Brothers will be discovered, although it seems unlikely. The following chart will aid the collector. The code letters are placed on the copyright page referring to month and year. Almost all Harper books since 1912 carry this code.

A—January	M—1912	Y—1924
B—February	N—1913	Z—1925
C—March	O—1914	A—1926
D—April	P—1915	B—1927
E—May	Q—1916	C—1928
F—June	R—1917	D—1929
G—July	S—1918	E—1930
H—August	T—1919	
I—September	U—1920	
K—October	V—1921	
L—November	W—1922	
M—December	X—1923	

NOTES

ADDENDA:
Literary Review of New York *Evening Post*, September 16, 1922. P. 23.
  Review of "One of Ours" (by Willa Cather) by Sinclair Lewis.

INDEX TO THE BIBLIOGRAPHY

INDEX TO THE BIBLIOGRAPHY

NOTE: Entries are given with bracketed numbers and letters indicating their place in the Bibliography as well as with page numbers; books by Sinclair Lewis are referred to in roman numerals (I–XXII), contributions to books in capital letters (A–P), uncollected writings in arabic numerals (1–211).

The Biographical and Critical Notices in Books and in Periodicals sections are not indexed; the former are arranged alphabetically; the latter chronologically.

"Adventures in Automobumming" (173), 166.
"Affinings of an Affinitist, The" (181), 155.
"Afterglow" (149), 163.
Advance issue, see DODSWORTH.
"Advertising, Lewis Looks at" (195), 169.
Ainslee's Magazine (124), 160.
"Alarm Clock, The" (46), 151.
"Ambrosial, Father" (8), 147.
Amenia, New York, 138.
"America, Can an Artist Live in" (191), 168.
America, criticism of (articles) (186, 187, 189, 190, 191, 194), 168–169.

"America, Self-Conscious" (190), 168.
"American Kiplings" (68), 153.
American Magazine (178, 180), 167.
American Mercury, 168.
AMERICAN SCRAP-BOOK, THE 1930
First edition (M), 141.
"American Views the Huns, An" (189), 168.
ARROWSMITH
First Edition (IX), 106.
First Trade Edition (X), 108.
Arrowsmith, Martin, 109.
"Art and the Woman" (59), 152.
"At Lighting Time" (30), 150.
"Authors and Interviewing" (184), 167.
"Awful Jungle, The" (99), 157.

BABBITT
First Edition (VIII), 102.
BABBITT, Points on First Issue of, 102.
"Babbitt, Be Brisk with" (188), 168.
Baker & Taylor, see *Christmas Bulletin*.
"Ballad from the City" (71), 154.
Baltimore *News* (126a), 160.
"Before Christmas" (90), 156.
"Behind the Arras" (15), 148.
Bellman, The, 160.
Benton, Charles E. (J), 138.
BEST SHORT STORIES OF 1918
First Edition (E), 133.
"Big Brother the Wise" (95), 157.
"Black Snow and Orange Sky" (146), 163.
Blanck, Jake, 102.
"Blind, Outlook for the" (117), 159.
Blue Mule, The (75), 154.
"Bongo" (205), 170.
Book News Monthly, 129, 159.
Book Review, see *International Book Review*.

INDEX TO THE BIBLIOGRAPHY

Book Reviews by Sinclair Lewis (117, 118, 119, 121, 126b).
Bookman, The (American) (127), 161.
"Books for the Class Room" (118), 159.
Bourget, Paul, 155.
Brattleboro, Vermont, 123, 143.
"Bronze Bars" (172), 166.
Bulletin, see San Francisco, *Christmas*.
"Butt, The" (102), 157.

Cabell, James Branch, 100, 134; see Future Publications, p. 84.
"California Lady, My" (93), 157.
"Can an Artist Live in America?" (191), 168.
"Canned Poetry" (50), 152.
"Canticle of Great Lovers, A" (124), 160.
"Carol, A Maytime" (4), 147.
"Cat of the Stars, The" (165), 165.
"Celtic Revival, The" (57), 152.
Century Magazine, 158, 167.
CHEAP AND CONTENTED LABOR, by Sinclair Lewis.
    First Edition (XVI), 116.
"Cherries of Providence," by Leo Larguier (78), 155.
"Christmas, Before" (90), 156.
Christmas Bulletin, Baker & Taylor's (130a), 161.
Circle, The, 155.
"Citizen of the Mirage" (182), 167.
"City Fountain, The" (97), 157.
"City Loneliness" (73), 154.
"City of Mercy" (209), 171.
"City Shadow" (112c), 159.
"Clergyman Who Fishes, The" (105), 158.
Cobb, Irvin S. (C), 131.
Cobb, Irvin S., HIS BOOK
    First Edition (C), 131.
"C-O-B-B," by Sinclair Lewis, 131.
Collier's Weekly, 110.
"Commutation $9.17" (129), 161.

"Complete Dialect Writer, The" (53), 152.
"Concerning Psychology" (17), 148.
Contributions to college periodicals, see Yale *Courant*, Yale
    Literary Magazine.
Cosmopolitan Magazine, 169, 170.
"Courage" (52), 152.
"Course in Heroism, A" (123), 160.
"Coward Minstrel, The" (5), 147.
"Cradle Song, The," by Von Liliencron (85), 156.
Critic, The, 135, 149.
"Crooning Lullaby, A" (34), 150.
"Curly Tailed Pup and Me" (47), 151.

"Dear Editor" (199), 169.
"Death-a-Cold, The" (108), 158.
"December Maying" (40), 151.
Delineator, The (108), 158.
"Dell, Floyd" (179), 167.
"Derelict, The," by Jean Reibrach (92), 156.
Designer, The, 158.
"Detour—Roads Rough" (154), 164.
"Devil Dog Rule" (203), 170.
"Dim Hours of Dusk" (69), 154.
"Disillusion" (89), 156.
"Display, Snappy" (143), 163.
DODSWORTH
    First Edition (XV), 114.
"Dollar Chasers" (211), 171.
Doran, Publishers, 132.
Dos Passos, John, 111.
"Down Here," by Sully Prudhomme (58), 152.
"Ecstasy," by Victor Hugo (67), 153.
"Editor's Table," see Yale *Literary Magazine*, 1906.
"Editors Who Write" (82), 155.
"Elementary Course in Erotics, An" (22), 149.
"Elizabeth, Kitty and Jane" (198), 169.
ELMER GANTRY

First Edition (XIII), 112.
"Enchanted Hour, The" (169), 166.
Every Week, 164.
Everybody's Magazine, 162.
"Exit Homo" (36), 150.
"Extracts from a Club-Woman's Diary" (63), 153.
"Faeries o' the Lake" (42), 151.
Famous Stories Magazine (reprints), 161, 166.
"Father Ambrosial" (8), 147.
"Father Kileen" (24), 149.
"Fireflies, The" (13), 148.
"Fireflies Grow, Where" (109), 158.
"Flocki, Remarkable Dog," by Presber (74), 154.
"Floyd Dell," by Sinclair Lewis (179), 167.
Foley, Charles (77), 155.
"For the Zelda Bunch" (147), 163.
"Fountain Spirit, The" (96), 157.
FOUR DAYS ON THE WEBUTUCK RIVER (J), 138.
FREE AIR
    First Edition (VI), 99.

"Gas Stove Beast, The" (48), 151.
"Gambler of the Night," by Bourget (79), 155.
"Getting His Bit" (158), 164.
"Ghost Patrol, The" (131), 161.
"Gladvertising" (161), 165.
"Gold in Umber" (94), 157.
Good Housekeeping, 163.
"Good Ship 'Teeter Board', The" (62), 153.
"Good Sport, The" (176), 166.
Graham, Tom (pseud. for Sinclair Lewis), 83, 91.
Gray Goose, The, 152.
Greis, Martin, 156.
Gruening, Ernest (H), 136.

"Habeas Corpus" (174), 166.
"Hack Driver, The" (185), 167.

"Hallowe'en" (7), 147.
"Hallowe'en" (80), 155.
Harper's Magazine, 167.
"He Had a Brother" (L), 140.
"He Loved His Country" (134), 162.
Hearst's International, see *Cosmopolitan* Magazine.
Hearst's Magazine, 163.
Herald Tribune, see New York *Herald Tribune*.
Hergesheimer, Joseph, 100, 144.
Herrmann, Eva (K), 139.
"Hidden People, The" (145), 163.
HIKE AND THE AEROPLANE
    First Edition (I), 91.
"Hippopotamus" (84), 155.
HISTORY OF CLASS OF 1907; YALE COLLEGE (B), 130.
"Hobohemia," see (139) and sequel (148).
    Dramatized and produced in New York, 1919.   Not published.
Holland's Magazine, 157.
Home Magazine, 155.
"Home Without Books, The" (130a), 161.
"Honestly if Possible" (135), 162.
Housekeeper, The, 150, 151, 153, 157.
Hugh Walpole, see Walpole, Hugh.
Hugo, Victor, 153.
Hutchins, Arthur, 91.

"If I Were Boss" (132), 161.
"I'm a Stranger Here Myself" (133), 161.
INNOCENTS, THE
    First Edition (V), 98.
International Book Review, 167.
"Invitation to Tea, An" (155), 164.
Irvin Cobb: His Book, see Cobb, Irvin.
"January Nights" (39), 151.
"Jazz" (160), 165.
JOB, THE

First Edition (IV), 96.
"Joy-Joy" (148), 163.
JURGEN AND THE CENSOR (F), 134.

Karlfeldt, Erik Axel, 118, 119, 120.
"Keep Out of the Kitchen" (201), 169.
Kennicott, Carol, The Story of, see MAIN STREET.
"Kidnapped Memorial, The" (168), 165.

Ladies' Home Journal, 164.
Ladies' World, 161.
"Lady's Maid, My" (104), 158.
"Land" (210), 171.
Larguier, Leo, 155.
LAUNCELOT (XXII), 125.
Lawrence, D. H., 160.
"Let's Play King" (207), 170.
"Letter from the Queen, A" (202), 170.
LETTER TO CRITICS
    First Edition (XX), 123.
"Lewis, Sinclair, Looks at Advertising" (195), 169.
Life, contributions to (55, 57, 61, 68, 82).
Limited edition of ARROWSMITH, 106.
Literary Digest (reprint), 153.
LITERARY TREASURES OF 1929
    First Edition (L), 140.
"Little Drummer of the Blues," by Foley, 155.
"Locki, the Red" (125), 160.
London, Jack, 83, 84, 124.
"Long Arm of the Small Town, The" (N), 142.
"Loneliness of Theodore, The" (23), 149.
Lorimer, George Horace, 169.

McClure's Magazine, 163, 164.
"Mæcenas Welches" (61), 153.
Magazine for the Blind, see *Volta Review*.
MAIN STREET
    First Edition (VII), 100.

"Main Street's Been Paved" (187), 168.

"Making Faces" (100), 157.

MAN WHO KNEW COOLIDGE, THE
First Edition (XIV), 113.

MANHATTAN TRANSFER, Lewis's Review of
First Edition (XII), 111.

MANTRAP
First Edition (XI), 110.

"Masque of Gaspar's Passing, The" (113), 159.

MASQUERADER, THE, 135, 149.

"Matsu-No-Kata" (25), 149.

"Matter of Business, A" (177), 167.

"May Afield" (54), 152.

"May Baskets" (98), 157.

"May Time Carol, A" (4), 147.

Mencken, H. L., 100, 112.

Mercury, see *American Mercury.*

Merrill, Stuart, 154.

Metropolitan Magazine, 162, 163, 164, 165.

"Might and Millions" (167), 165.

Minneapolis *Journal* (192a), 168.

Minnesota, 142.

"Minnesota, The Norse State" (H), 136.

"Miracle Forsooth, A" (18), 148.

MITCHELL, JOHN AMES (A), 129.

"Moon of Night," by Greis (87), 156.

Morand, Paul, 103, 104.

"Moths in the Arc Light" (162), 165.

"Mr. Lorimer and Me" (193), 169.

"Murder, The Post-Mortem" (181), 167.

MY MAIDEN EFFORT (G), 135.

"My Policeman" (112), 158.

"Mystery, The" (103), 157.

Nation, The, 136, 167, 168, 169, 170.

"Nature, Inc." (128), 161.

Nautilus, The, 158, 159.

"Ne'er-Do-Weel, A" (16), 148.
New Age, The, 152, 157.
New England Magazine, 153.
New Idea (Woman's Magazine), 156.
New Orleans *Times-Democrat*, 154.
New Statesman, 168.
New York *Herald-Tribune*, 168.
"Nimrod, Junior" (64), 153.
NOBEL PRIZE ADDRESS
    First Edition (XVII), 118.
    Revised Edition (XVIII), 120.
    First Separate Edition (XIX), 122.
"Noble Experiment, A" (204), 170.
Now and Then, 167.
"Number Seven to Sagapoose" (180), 167.

O'Brien, Edward J., 133.
"Odysseus at Ogygia" (6), 148.
ON PARADE
    First Edition (K), 139.
"One Takes His Ease" (115), 159.
Open Court, The, 158.
OPINIONS ON AMENITIES OF BOOK COLLECTING (P), 144.
O-SA-GE, THE
    First Edition (N), 142.
"Other Side of the House, The" (130), 161.
OUR MR. WRENN
    First Edition (II), 93.
Outer's Book, The, 151, 152, 153, 154, 158.
"Outer's Song, The" (72), 154.
"Outlook for the Blind, The" (117), 159.
Overland Monthly, 157.

Pacific Monthly, 149, 156.
"Passage in Isaiah, A" (56), 152.
"Passing of Capitalism, The" (127), 161.
"Passing Pantomime, The" (66), 153.

Peach, Arthur Wallace (O), 143.
Peoples' Magazine (110), 158.
Pictorial Review, 141, 165.
"Pleasure Cure, San Francisco's" (116), 159.
Poems in German (2, 9), 147, 148.
"Poinsettia Widow, The" (137), 162.
"Policeman, My" (112), 158.
"Polly" (114), 159.
Popular Magazine (161), 165.
Posselt, Erich (K), 139.
"Post-Mortem Murder, The" (181), 167.
"Praise of South Middle, In" (37), 150.
Preface to French Edition of BABBITT, 103, 104.
Presber, Rudolf (74), 154.
"Protoplasm and the Soul" (119), 159.
Prudhomme, Sully (58), 152.
"Publicity Gone Mad" (194), 169.
Puck, contributions to, 152, 153, 155, 157, 160.
"Puck to Queen Mab" (3), 147.
Pulitzer Prize Committee, Letter to (192), 168.

"Quatrain, The" (65), 153.

"Raking of the Rakers, A" (55), 152.
Red Book Magazine, 151, 158, 166, 167.
Reibrach, Jean (92), 156.
"Return to America, I" (186), 168.
"Review of Reviewers, A" (183), 167.
"Ring Around a Rosy" (208), 170.
"Rondeau of Farewell, A" (49), 152.
"Rondeau of Sorrow, A" (56a), 152.
"Rose for Little Eva, A" (152), 164.
Rotary Club address, 143.
Rugg, Harold Goddard (O), 143.

"Saint Hubert" (27), 149.
St. Louis *Republic* (120b), 160.
San Francisco *Bulletin* (112b, 113), 158, 160.

"San Francisco's Pleasure Cure" (116), 159.

Saturday Evening Post, 133, 161, 162, 163, 164, 165, 166, 170, 171.

Saturday Review of Literature (XII), 111.

"Scarlet Sign, The" (140), 162.

"Scented Spring and the G. P." (126), 160.

Scripps-Howard Newspapers, 116.

"Sea of Cities, The" by Von Liliencron (76), 154.

"Seventh Troop, The" (11), 148.

"Shadowy Glass, The" (156), 164.

"Shore, The," by Theodore Storm (85), 155.

SHORT STORIES
    First Edition, 137.

Short Stories Magazine (125, 126), 160.

"Shrimp-Coloured Blouse, The" (171), 166.

"Shrinking Violet, The" (162), 165.

"Singing Men, The" (126c), 161.

"Sleepy Head Top" (43), 151.

"Slip It to 'Em" (153), 164.

Smart Set Magazine, 153, 154, 156, 161.

"Smile Lady, The" (112a), 158.

"Snappy Display" (143), 163.

"Snare, The," by Paul Bourget (88), 156.

"Song of the King's Jester, The," by Merrill (70), 154.

"Song of Prince Hal, A" (1), 147.

"Sons and Lovers," by Lawrence, review of (126b), 160.

Special advance issue, see DODSWORTH.

"Speed" (170), 166.

"Spirit's Call, The" (107), 158.

"Spiritualist Vaudeville" (151), 164.

"Stars and Stripes" (M), 141.

Sterling, George, 84.

Storm, Theodore (83), 155.

"Story with a Happy Ending, A" (138), 162.

"Stranger Here Myself, I'm a" (133), 161.

"Struggle, The" (86), 156.

"Student Lied" (2), 147.

"Summer in Winter" (110), 158.
"Summer's Tale, A" (20), 149.
Sunset Magazine (114, 115, 116), 159.
Suppression of First Edition of Nobel Prize Address (XVII), 118.
"Swept Hearth, The" (159), 164.

"Tamarack Lover" (150), 163.
Taylor, Harvey, 84, 124, 126.
"Tether Ball" (106), 138.
"Theory of Values, A" (28), 149.
"There Was a Prince" (196), 169.
THESE UNITED STATES
   First Edition (H), 136.
"They That Take the Sword" (111), 158.
"Things" (164), 165.
"Third Estate, The" (10), 148.
Thompson, Dorothy (Mrs. Sinclair Lewis) (M), 141.
Thurston, Mrs., see under Zangwill.
"Tour of England" (192a), 168.
Tower Magazine (reprint) (150), 163.
TRAIL OF THE HAWK, THE
   First Edition (III), 94.
Transatlantic Tales, 152, 153, 154, 155, 156.
Translations by Sinclair Lewis, see *Transatlantic Tales*.
Troutbeck Press (J), 138.
Tully, Thomas A. (B), 130.
"Twenty-Four Hours in June" (136), 162.
"Two Writing Manuals" (120), 160.

"Ultra-Modern, The" (60), 153.
"Um Ein und Zwanzig" (9), 148.
United Feature Syndicate, 116.
United States, These, see THESE UNITED STATES.
"Unknown Undergraduates" (32), 150.

VALLEY OF THE MOON, by Sinclair Lewis.
   First Edition (XXI), 124.

"Vaudeville, Spiritualist" (151), 164.
VERMONT PROSE, First Edition, (O), 143.
Volta Review, 159, 160.
Von Liliencron, Detlev, (76, 85) 154, 156.

"Wailing and Fixing of Teeth" (101), 157.
Walpole, Hugh (D), 132.
"Wash Bowl Sea, On" (91), 156.
"Watcher Across the Road, The" (166), 165.
"Way I See It, The" (175), 166.
"Way to Rome, The" (122), 160.
WEBUTUCK RIVER, FOUR DAYS ON THE (J), 138.
"What a Man!" (200), 169.
"When Viziers Speak" (14), 148.
"Where Fireflies Grow" (109), 158.
"Whisperer, The" (144), 163.
Who Is Hugh Walpole? (D), 132.
"Widower for A While, A" (157), 164.
Wiggin, Kate Douglas (126b), 160.
"William Butler Yeats, To" (75), 154.
"Willow Walk, The" (E), 133.
"Woman by the Candle Light, A" (142), 162.
Woman's Home Companion (39, 46, 99), 151, 157.
Woman's Magazine, see *New Idea*.
Wrenn, Our Mr., see OUR MR. WRENN.

YALE COLLEGE, HISTORY OF THE CLASS OF 1907 (B), 130.
"Yeats, William Butler, To" (75), 154.
"Yellow Streak, The" (19), 148.
"Young Man Axelbrod" 137.
"Young Man, Go East" (206), 170.
"Youth" (203a), 170.
Youth's Companion (90), 156.

Zangwill, Israel, 135, 149.
"Zelda Bunch, For the" (147), 163.
"Zenata" (121), 160.